The Monetary versus Fiscal Policy Debate

The
Monetary versus Fiscal Policy Debate

Lessons from Two Decades

Edited by

R. W. Hafer

ROWMAN & ALLANHELD
PUBLISHERS

ROWMAN & ALLANHELD

Published in the United States of America in 1986
by Rowman & Allanheld, Publishers
(a division of Littlefield, Adams & Company)
81 Adams Drive, Totowa, New Jersey 07512

Library of Congress Cataloging in Publication Data
Main entry under title:

The Monetary versus fiscal policy debate.

Papers presented at a conference held Oct. 12-13, 1984,
sponsored by the Federal Reserve Bank of St. Louis.
    Includes bibliographies and index.
    1. Monetary policy—Congresses.   2. Fiscal policy—
Congresses.   I. Hafer, R. W.   II. Federal Reserve
Bank of St. Louis.
HG230.3.M64   1986   339.5′2   85-11912
ISBN 0-8476-7454-1

86 87 88 / 10 9 8 7 6 5 4 3 2 1
Printed in the United States of America

Contents

Preface and Acknowledgments

The selection of this conference topic provides an opportunity to honor Homer Jones, director of research at the Federal Reserve Bank of St. Louis from 1958 to 1971. Although some students of the monetary versus fiscal policy debate may not recognize the name, Homer's influence on the topics discussed in this volume is substantial. As director of research, Homer was instrumental in the development of the St. Louis Fed's statistical publications that provide current information on the important monetary and financial measures. His intellectual prodding of the research staff to investigate various aspects of monetary theory and policy, and his encouragement to report their findings in the Bank's *Review* and in scholarly journals helped to contribute to our understanding of the effects of monetary policy actions on the economy. In appreciation for his efforts, we gladly dedicate this conference volume to Homer Jones.

Many people associated with the Research and Public Information Department at the Federal Reserve Bank of St. Louis contributed to the planning of the conference upon which this volume is based. In particular, I would like to thank Dan Brennan, Melissa Daubach, and Linda Moser for their assistance. I also would like to thank Spencer Carr of Rowman & Allanheld for his help in the production of this book.

The Monetary versus Fiscal Policy Debate

1

Introduction

R.W. Hafer
FEDERAL RESERVE BANK OF ST. LOUIS

From October 12 to 13, 1984, the Federal Reserve Bank of St. Louis held its ninth annual economic policy conference. The topic of this conference was "The Monetary versus Fiscal Policy Debate: Lessons from Two Decades." This volume consists of papers and comments presented at that conference.

The debate among economists about the relative usefulness of monetary or fiscal policy actions has taken many forms over the past 20 years. The policy discussion began with a small number of studies showing that money growth was more reliably related to income growth than autonomous consumption. Today, it encompasses a vast body of empirical research, including recent investigations into the channels by which policy effects are transmitted to the economy.

The nature of the monetary versus fiscal policy debate generally has been an empirical matter. The relative ease with which one can substitute various policy measures to test their impact on economic activity has attracted many scholars. As a result, conferences such as this usually have been replete with regression output that pits one version of the so-called St. Louis equation against another.

In the papers assembled for this conference, we have explicitly avoided yet another confrontation between competing regression results. Rather, the intent of this conference was to stand back and examine the impact of the debate on the general direction of macroeconomic theory from alternative perspectives. The central theme around which the papers were built is the question "What have we learned?"

Part I of the book focuses on the development of the debate by investigating different technical aspects and the changes with regard to the basic theoretical issues. Part II examines the development of fiscal policy analysis during the past two decades. Part III contains papers that view the debate differently from the norm—namely, from public choice and rational expectations perspectives.

Part I

In "Monetary versus Fiscal Policy Effects: A Review of the Debate," Bennett T. McCallum, professor of economics at Carnegie-Mellon University, explores several key technical issues that have developed since the late 1960s. Focusing on the arguments raised against the reduced-form approach to measuring the relative impact of monetary and fiscal actions on nominal GNP, McCallum notes that an issue of continuing interest concerns the possible endogeneity of policy actions. Because such endogeneity may produce distorted empirical estimates of policy effectiveness, McCallum provides some preliminary empirical estimates based on procedures that attempt to reduce this effect. In doing so he finds that the summed effect of the money growth coefficients is about one, and that the cumulative value of the fiscal coefficients is approximately zero. The author argues that further work in this area should attempt to investigate the endogenous policy effects that may influence empirical estimates.

McCallum also reviews the conflicting evidence about the relative size of the monetary and fiscal policy multipliers, the evidence obtained by comparing the small reduced-form model results to those derived from large, multiequation macro models, and recent evidence from vector autoregression (VAR) models. In general, he argues that the evidence does not refute the contention that monetary actions are more important than fiscal actions in explaining the behavior of nominal and real GNP. Moreover, McCallum demonstrates that, in a Ricardian economy in which individuals incorporate the government's budget constraint in their future saving–consumption plans, a money-financed increase (decrease) in expenditures (taxes) stimulates aggregate demand more than a bond-financed increase.

Part II

Karl Brunner, director of the Center for Research in Government Policy and Business and professor of economics at the University of Rochester, provides an extensive analysis of the evolution of fiscal policy analysis during the past two decades in his paper "Fiscal Policy in Macro Theory: A Survey and Evaluation." Using the multiplier effects on aggregate demand and economic activity, he traces this evolution from the early discussions that focused on the impact of fiscal actions. This view, which dominated the professional macroeconomic literature during the 1940s and 1950s, was challenged by the perception of market failure inherent in the Keynesian view and by early monetarist work that presented empirical analyses of the relative impacts of fiscal and monetary impulses on the economy.

Brunner notes that this early empirical testing demonstrated the confusion over the appropriate implementation of theoretical Keynesian stabilization policies. The "reduced-form" equations approach, Brunner asserts, was a useful step in empirically testing competing hypotheses. As he notes, the evidence did not directly test the income—expenditure framework per se, but it provided a useful way of testing hypotheses that emerge directly from that framework. This empirical assault on Keynesian policy prescriptions of the pre-1960s clearly altered the notions that fiscal policy is the active component of stabilization policy, and that monetary policy plays only an accommodative role in the context of an interest rate strategy.

Although the monetary versus fiscal actions debate continues, the extent of the empirical charges and countercharges has diminished considerably from its late 1960s level. This, Brunner notes, results from a more general acceptance of the role of money as the dominant impulse in policy actions. More significant, however, in terms of the change in fiscal policy analysis, is the recent emergence of the "neoclassical" contribution to policy analysis.

Brunner extensively evaluates the emergence and impact of the rational expectations approach on the profession's perception of the significance of government actions. Citing the influential work of Robert Barro, he also examines the nature and relevance of the so-called Ricardian theme. Although Brunner acknowledges the clear limitations of this approach, he recognizes that it has opened a new dimension into fiscal analysis. In this context, the recent increased interest, both public and professional, in fiscal processes stems from this research agenda.

In concluding his paper, Brunner raises the concern about the efficacy of an activist policy. Although our knowledge has progressed from that of two decades ago, he argues that we still do not possess adequate information about the dynamic interrelationships that exist in the economy. Moreover, echoing an idea expressed by James Buchanan (see Chapter 5), he asserts that it is not clear that such knowledge would be sufficient to yield socially successful policy actions. Fiscal activism, Brunner concludes, may well produce inefficiencies greater than those that the policies were designed to control.

In commenting on Brunner's paper, Alan S. Blinder, professor of economics at Princeton University, argues that the depiction of Keynesian theory as disdainful of the effect of monetary impulses is inaccurate. Recalling his undergraduate days at Princeton in the early 1960s and citing from Samuelson's text for support, Blinder contends that monetary policy and money were in fact viewed as important by Keynesian macro theories of that time.

Blinder also argues that the notion that simple correlation analysis provides an effective hypothesis testing procedure can only hold under very restrictive conditions. This criticism applies to the use of reduced-form type of models in which nominal income is explained by fiscal and monetary actions. If the policy measures are orthogonal, then one may decompose the variance of income growth into the variances of fiscal actions, monetary actions, and an error term. Once fiscal and monetary policies are set by policymakers to offset movements in income, however, this orthogonality condition does not hold. Because of the covariance between fiscal and monetary actions, estimates of each policy tool's effect on income may be grossly inaccurate.

On the issues of the government budget constraint and the Ricardian equivalence theorem, Blinder generally agrees with much of Brunner's analysis. He does argue, however, that there is evidence that, properly estimated, the monetary authority does "monetize the deficit." His analysis of the data suggests that larger deficits do cause faster growth in back reserves, although the effect is relatively small in magnitude.

Robert J. Gordon, professor of economics at Northwestern University, also provides comments on Brunner's paper. Like Blinder, Gordon argues that Brunner's description of the early monetary versus fiscal policy debate is misleading. Gordon notes that the evolution of the policy prescriptions should not be studied without explicit reference to the events of the time. For example, he cites the weak economic recovery occurring during a period of rapid money growth during the late 1930s that discredited the role of monetary policy among many economists. Also citing from one of Samuelson's early editions, Gordon produces numerous quotes to support his contention that monetary policy was not ignored by early Keynesians. The declining importance of activists' fiscal policy arguments and the rise of monetary policy's importance during the late 1960s and early 1970s also reflect the events of time and supporting empirical evidence: the growing importance of the Friedman—Phelps natural rate hypothesis and the empirical results reported by Andersen and Jordan are two mentioned in the discussion.

Gordon also finds the importance placed by Brunner on reduced-form spending equations to be curious. He references the work of Blinder and Goldfeld and his own research wherein the estimated coefficients derived from standard "St. Louis equations" are shown to be biased. In this vein he reports that some of his recent research suggests that there is empirical support for the notion that innovations in the money supply and autonomous innovations in structures investment have an impact on the business cycle.

In his comments on Brunner's Ricardian equivalence theory discussion, Gordon takes the position that much of the empirical work, using reduced-form consumption equations, on this question is unlikely to provide reliable evidence. Some of his objections to such estimations include the following: the inclusion of government spending and tax revenues as explanatory variables resurrects the Goldfeld and Blinder criticism; such equations generally do not properly account for lags between changes in taxes and spending; there is no distinction between permanent and temporary tax changes; and more. With these criticisms, Gordon argues that Brunner's emphasis on these tests seems misplaced.

Part III

The papers that make up the third part of this book provide an alternative view to assess the successes and failures of the monetary versus fiscal policy debate. In his paper "Can Policy Activism Succeed? A Public Choice Perspective," James M. Buchanan, director of the Center for Study of Public Choice and professor of economics at George Mason University, poses the question "Can any activist policy, monetary or fiscal, succeed within the existing institutional–constitutional framework?" He points out that concepts of "success" and "failure" in macroeconomic policy require some preconceived notion of society's preference for certain policy outcomes. Even under the most simple of models, however, Buchanan concludes that policies most often will be deemed failures by society.

This viewpoint is based on the notion that, in the absence of a well-defined set of rules establishing policy parameters, policymakers are likely to be more responsive to pressure for short-term rather than long-term solutions. In this vein, Buchanan notes that the removal of viable constraints on the actions of monetary authorities under a pure fiat money regime produces predictable outcomes of expansionary policy actions.

Buchanan's analysis of the setting of monetary and fiscal policy leads him to conclude that unless institutional–constitutional constraints can be enacted, the success of macroeconomic policy is doubtful. In the area of fiscal policy he contends that the reduction or removal of budgetary manipulation precedes a genuine hope for achieving success in macroeconomic policy. In this context he makes an argument for the constitutional rule enforcing a balanced budget. Similarly, Buchanan argues that monetary policymakers' discretionary power also should be limited by binding policy rules, such as Milton Friedman's money growth rule, a price rule, or a rule based on a self-regulating commodity base.

In the last chapter, John Taylor, professor of economics at Stanford University, presents a rational expectations outlook of the debate in his paper "An Appeal for Rationality in the Policy Activism Debate." Taylor notes that, during the past decade, the monetary versus fiscal policy debate was largely supplanted by the so-called policy ineffectiveness debate. Essentially based on discussions of the models of Lucas, Sargent and Wallace, and Barro, the policy debate evolved from the monetary versus fiscal policy issue to the issue of whether any policy could be effective in manipulating macroeconomic variables when economic agents are rational. As this debate progressed, it was discovered that the policy ineffectiveness results were based on certain assumptions in these models.

The effect of these findings, Taylor notes, was to turn the discussion away from the issue of policy ineffectiveness and back to the numerous remaining areas of the debate. For example, how does one deal with the problem of lags and uncertainty? How does one implement an activist policy rule? Although these (and other) issues remain unresolved, Taylor argues that the current state of the policy activism debate is one in which there is no operational structure specific enough to be used in resolving disagreements. In this context he suggests that the rational expectations approach, which the author outlines in five general principles, could provide such a suitable framework to evaluate alternative policies.

Part I

Technical and Theoretical Issues in the Evolution of the Monetary versus Fiscal Policy Debate

2

Monetary versus Fiscal Policy Effects: A Review of the Debate

Bennett T. McCallum
CARNEGIE-MELLON UNIVERSITY
AND NATIONAL BUREAU OF ECONOMIC RESEARCH

1. Introduction

The "monetary versus fiscal policy" debate has not attracted much attention in recent years, and, in some ways, this is not to be regretted. It may therefore be useful to begin this discussion with a quote from Phillip Cagan (1978, 85–86):

> No one who was not in touch with the economics profession in the 1940s and 1950s can quite imagine the state of thinking then in the profession at large on monetary theory and policy. The quantity of money was not considered important, indeed was hardly worth mentioning, for questions of aggregate demand, unemployment, and even inflation ... Textbooks in basic economics and even in money and banking mentioned the quantity theory of money, if at all, only to hold it up to ridicule. Those textbooks produced an entire cohort of professional economists who became the teachers of hordes of economics students. There were, of course, many exceptions, most notably at the University of Chicago ... But if you traveled among the profession at large, mention of the quantity of money elicited puzzled glances of disbelief or sly smiles of condescension.

As a former member of the horde of students that Cagan refers to, I would modify his statement only by suggesting that the period in question lasted longer than he indicates. For readers who find this claim hard to

The author is indebted to Carl Christ, Stanley Fischer, Robert King, Thomas Mayer, Lawrence Meyer, and Allan Meltzer for helpful comments and to the National Science Foundation (SES 84-08691) for financial assistance.

believe, I would suggest perusal of the contents of the American
Economic Association's *Readings in Business Cycles,* published in 1965
(Gordon and Klein 1965). Another interesting record is provided by the
chapter on inflation in Ackley (1961), the standard, graduate macro text of
the 1960s. Ackley begins with a brief description of the "classical school"
theory in which inflation depends primarily upon growth of the quantity
of money, but quickly moves on to other ideas.[1]

Today, of course, matters are different. There are few economists who
would label themselves "monetarists," but most publishing macroeconomists hold views that would have been two standard deviations away from
the mean—in the monetarist direction—in 1965. As one piece of evidence
in support of that claim, I would point to the specifications (i.e., list of
variables) of vector autoregression (VAR) models currently being used for
forecasting and/or analysis. In particular, the VAR systems of Sims
(1980, 1982), Litterman (1982), Gordon and King (1982), Webb (1984),
and B. M. Friedman (1984) all include monetary aggregates but no fiscal
variables.

Both sides in the debate can of course claim victory: the monetary policy supporters for the reasons implicit in the foregoing comparison, and
the fiscal policy supporters by citing theory and evidence indicating that
fiscal actions are not without effect on aggregate demand. But the shift
has certainly been in favor of the former.

The purpose of this paper is to review developments bearing on this
debate over the last 20 years. To describe all of the significant items in
the literature would require a paper of inordinate length and one that
would be extremely dull for the participants at this conference, most of
whom are intimately familiar with much of the material. Fortunately, it
turns out to be unnecessary for me to provide an extensive treatment of
the main threads of the argument, for a careful review was published
fairly recently by Meyer and Rasche (1980). I will be able, then, to pass
quickly through the well-known items and arguments and focus my attention on items that (i) have been neglected, (ii) are fairly recent, or (iii) are
somewhat original. The organization of the paper is very simple: Section
2 is concerned with empirical studies and econometric points of interpretation, Section 3 discusses some of the main theoretical issues, and Section
4 provides some tentative conclusions and judgments.

2. Empirical Results and Econometric Issues

2.1 Single-equation results

In discussing the empirical analysis and related issues, it is convenient to
organize the discussion around results featured in a long series of articles
prepared by the research department of the Federal Reserve Bank of St.

Louis.[2] Brief mention should be made, however, of the earlier paper by Friedman and Meiselman (1963), which is not discussed by Meyer and Rasche.

The central ingredient of the Friedman–Meiselman study was a comparison of simple correlations (based on annual U.S. data for 1897–1958 and subperiods) of consumption with money stock magnitudes, on the one hand, and consumption with "autonomous" fiscal variables,[3] on the other hand. Friedman and Meiselman found that movements in consumption were more highly correlated with monetary rather than fiscal variations. Their own summary statement goes as follows:

> The results are strikingly one-sided. Except for the early years of the Great Depression, money . . . is more closely related to consumption than is autonomous expenditures . . . . This is so both for nominal values . . . and for "real" values . . . . It is true both for absolute values and for year-to-year or quarter-to-quarter changes. Such correlation as there is between autonomous expenditures and consumption is in the main a disguised reflection of the common effect of money on both . . . . One implication of the results is that the critical variable for monetary policy is the stock of money, not interest rates or investment expenditures. (1963, 166)

Given the climate described by Cagan, the central role of the consumption function in Keynesian analysis, and some questionable methodology, the Friedman–Meiselman study was welcomed by the profession about like an unexpected slap in the face. Strongly critical studies were published by Hester (1964), Ando and Modigliani (1965), and DePrano and Mayer (1965). Strongly worded replies and rejoinders of great length followed promptly.

It is clear that the Friedman–Meiselman approach was in fact open to several methodological objections. Its critics emphasized the questionable nature of the measure used for autonomous expenditures as well as the delineation of sample subperiods. Especially troublesome was the focus on contemporaneous relationships in single regression equations including only one or two explanatory variables. Most researchers in macroeconomics believed, I would guess, that investigation of the issues under discussion could be adequately carried out in the context of a fully specified, simultaneous-equation, econometric model. The judgment of Blinder and Solow (1974, 65), expressed a few years later, was that "all of this was essentially pointless. The issue is simply not to be settled by comparing goodness of fit of one-equation models that are far too primitive to represent *any* theory adequately."

Thus the Friedman–Meiselman results were in the process of being shrugged off when the first of the St. Louis studies—that of Andersen and Jordan (1968)—appeared. As is very well known, that study featured a least squares regression fit to quarterly U.S. data for 1952.1–1968.2 in which the dependent variable was the change in nominal GNP, and the explanatory variables were current and lagged values of changes in the money stock (M1 or base), full-employment expenditures, and full-employment tax receipts. The striking finding was that the sum of the coefficients on the monetary variable was highly significant, whereas the sum of the coefficients on both fiscal variables was insignificantly different from zero.[4]

2.2. Econometric objections

Again, sharply critical objections were raised. The main lines of argument were brought together by Blinder and Solow (1974) and nicely reviewed by Meyer and Rasche (1980). My strategy here will be to focus on three points emphasized by Blinder and Solow (see below) and on the evidence concerning reliability of "reduced-form" procedures that was subsequently described by Modigliani and Ando (1976). It will be convenient, though, to begin by quickly mentioning the observation of Benjamin Friedman (1977) that when data for the period 1970.1–1976.2 is added to the Andersen–Carlson (1970) sample, the sum of the fiscal variable coefficients becomes significantly positive. It was quickly shown by Carlson (1978), however, that this conclusion does not obtain when the variables are entered in rate-of-change form rather than as first differences. In effect, Carlson's suggested specification amount to

$$\Delta y_t = \alpha + \beta(L)\Delta m_t + \gamma(L)\Delta g_t + u_t, \qquad (1)$$

where y_t, m_t, and g_t are logarithms of nominal GNP, a money stock measure, and a fiscal variable, respectively; u_t is a stochastic disturbance, and $\beta(L)$ and $\gamma(L)$ denote finite polynomials in the lag operator defined by $L^n x_t = x_{t-n}$, so that $\beta(L)\Delta m_t$ stands for a distributed lag such as $\beta_0 \Delta m_t + \beta_1 \Delta m_{t-1} + \cdots + \beta_k \Delta m_{t-k}$. Carlson's specification not only has the desirable feature of relating relative rather than absolute changes, but it also leads to residuals that are more consistent with the standard assumption that u_t is a white-noise disturbance.[5] Consequently, (1) seems preferable to the specification used previously, and this judgment leads to the conclusion that the inclusion of data for years since 1969 does not reverse the original finding that the sum of the γ_j coefficients is insignificantly different from zero. In what follows I will accordingly presume that (1) is the relevant specification.

Let us now consider, then, the criticisms of Blinder and Solow (1974). Those writers summarize their position very concisely as follows:

> In summary, the Andersen–Jordan study errs for at least three reasons, any one of which is sufficient to render their results meaningless. First, by omit-

ting all exogenous variables other than fiscal or monetary policy, they seriously misspecify the reduced-form equation for real [*sic*] output . . . . Second, they use an incorrect measure of fiscal policy, which biases the coefficient toward zero. Finally, and most damaging to their position, they treat fiscal and monetary policies as exogenous when it is intuitively obvious that the authorities are in some sense reacting to movements in the macroeconomy. (pp. 70–71)

These three difficulties correspond to those discussed by Meyer and Rasche (1980, 56–63) and Batten and Thornton (1983, n. 2). We will take them in turn, starting with the omission of exogenous variables. In this case the contention is that the true specification is not (1) but

$$\Delta y_t = \alpha + \beta(L)\Delta m_t + \gamma(L)\Delta g_t + \delta(L)\Delta z_t + u_t, \qquad (2)$$

where z_t is an additional variable[6] that has an important influence on y_t. For the moment, let us suppose that Δm_t and Δg_t are in fact exogenous, a supposition that will be considered later in connection with the third difficulty. Now Blinder and Solow refer to z_t as an *exogenous* variable. But the conditions for true statistical exogeneity are extremely stringent: z_t must be generated by a process that is independent of current and past values of y_t (and thus u_t). But it is hard to imagine any important macroeconomic variable that is truly exogenous in that sense; even population growth and technical change probably respond (with lags) to fluctuations in GNP.[7] The point is better expressed, then, as suggesting that (2) is applicable with Δz_t interpreted as an endogenous variable that is affected by Δy_t, Δm_t, and Δg_t only with a lag. Suppose that relation is

$$\Delta z_t = a_0 + a_1\Delta y_{t-1} + a_2\Delta m_{t-1} + a_3\Delta g_{t-1} + \xi_t, \qquad (3)$$

where ξ_t is a stochastic disturbance term. Then by substitution and rearrangement we have

$$\Delta y_t = [\alpha + \delta(L)a_0] + [\beta(L) + a_2L\delta(L)]\Delta m_t \qquad (4)$$

$$+ [\gamma(L) + a_3L\delta(L)]\Delta g_t + a_1\delta(L)\Delta y_{t-1} + [u_t + \delta(L)\xi_t],$$

which is not in the form of (2) because of the appearance of $a_1\delta(L)y_{t-1}$. That can be remedied, however, by moving the Δy_{t-1} term to the left side and multiplying through by $[1 - La_1\delta(L)]^{-1}$:

$$\Delta y_t = \alpha' + \beta'(L)\Delta m_t + \gamma'(L)\Delta g_t + u'_t. \qquad (5)$$

Here we have a relation of the form of (2), but (of course) with disturbances and parameters that are quite different:

$$\beta' = [1 - La_1\delta(L)]^{-1} [\beta(L) + a_2L\delta(L)]$$

$$\gamma' = [1 - La_1\delta(L)]^{-1} [\gamma(L) + a_3L\delta(L)]$$

$$u'_t = [1 - La_1\delta(L)]^{-1} [u_t + \delta(L)\xi_t].$$

What we have in (5) is not a reduced-form equation but a *final-form* equation for Δy_t (still assuming that Δm_t and Δg_t are truly exogenous).[8]

Thus we see that the coefficients in (5), which will be estimated by the St. Louis procedure, are not the reduced-form coefficients in (1). The estimated values will, under the assumption that $\delta(L) \neq 0$ in (2) and that (3) is a "stable" relationship, reflect indirect influences of Δm_t and Δg_t on Δy_t by way of Δz_t. But the importance of that observation is quite unclear; the coefficients in a reduced-form equation like (1) also reflect influences that are "indirect." The first problem mentioned by Blinder and Solow hardly justifies, then, terming the St. Louis estimates "meaningless." It merely implies that in interpreting the estimates it may be necessary to keep in mind that they reflect "indirect" effects.[9]

It should be added that the foregoing argument presumes that Eq. (3) is "stable"—that is, unchanging over the sample period. Such relationships may in fact change significantly over real-time sample periods, for reasons explained by Lucas (1976) or for other reasons. But precisely the same must be said for (1); these two relationships are on the same footing in that respect. If there is reason to believe that (1) is stable over a period, there is no particular reason to expect (3) to be shifting.

Let us turn next to the second of the Blinder–Solow (1974) points—that the St. Louis measures of fiscal policy may be "incorrect." This means that the St. Louis variable does not correspond to the "weighted standardized surplus" shown by Blinder and Solow (1974, 23, 33–34) to be the measure that would appear in a reduced-form expression within *the particular model* that they use for illustrative purposes. But this is a conclusive criticism only to one who has some attachment to the particular model in question,[10] and then only if he believes that the effect of using alternative measures would be large. Although Corrigan (1970) found that a specific measure, which Blinder and Solow consider reasonably attractive, led to estimates indicating a significant fiscal effect, it is my impression that the variable measurement problem is not of overwhelming importance empirically. Or, to put it differently, if there is a fiscal policy measure that carries a strongly significant sum of coefficients in an equation of the St. Louis form, its existence has not been well publicized.[11] In any event, analysis of the policy-variable measurement issue is undermined by the third problem discussed by Blinder and Solow, to which we now turn.

The issue in this case results from the endogeneity of policy actions, a topic that was investigated in detail by Goldfeld and Blinder (1972). The Goldfeld–Blinder paper correctly emphasizes the distinction between exogeneity, in the sense of coming from outside the private sector of the economy and exogeneity in the statistical sense. And they note that it is almost inconceivable that either the monetary or the fiscal variables in the St. Louis studies could be exogenous in the latter sense, for that would imply that the authorities' actions are not systematically influenced to any significant extent by current or past macroeconomic conditions. If in fact the authorities' actions are so influenced, then (2) may not be a proper reduced-form equation even if no variables are omitted. In particular, the disturbance term u_t will be correlated with regressor variables if policy actions respond to current-quarter conditions, or if policy responds with a lag but the disturbance in (1) is autocorrelated. Under such circumstances, least squares estimates of $\beta(L)$ and $\gamma(L)$ will of course be biased and inconsistent.

This point is clearly correct in principle and could easily be of importance empirically.[12] The numbers reported in Goldfeld and Blinder's Table 8 suggest, however, that the downward bias should be about the same for monetary variable coefficients as for fiscal variable coefficients, except in the event that the fiscal authorities are extremely prompt and accurate in their stabilization efforts. It seems unlikely that this would be the case for the U.S. economy.

Nevertheless, the point is important enough to warrant continued discussion. Given that the policy authorities do respond to current or recent macroeconomic conditions, the best way to proceed in estimating equations like (1) or (5) is to append policy-rule or reaction-function specifications for the authorities and carry out simultaneous equation estimation, as recommended by Goldfeld and Blinder. But it is not *necessary* to explicitly formulate equations descriptive of policy behavior; consistent estimates of (5) can be obtained by estimating that equation in isolation but using instrumental variables (IV) rather than ordinary least squares (OLS) estimators. Comparisons of IV and OLS results should indicate whether severe biases are in fact induced by the reactive behavior of the policy authorities.

The results of an extremely brief and tentative exploration of that type are reported in Table 2.1. The first pair of numerical columns gives coefficient and standard error values for an OLS regression of the form of (5), using quarterly data on nominal GNP, the M1 money supply, and nominal federal purchases of goods and services for 1954–80. Despite the absence of polynomial constraints and the use of a different expenditure variable, the results are much like those that have been featured in the St. Louis studies. In particular, the Δm_{t-j} variables are strongly significant

Table 2.1
OLS vs. IV Estimates of St. Louis Equations
Sample Period: 1954.1 - 1980.4

Regressor	OLS Estimates		IV Estimates*	
	Coef.	(SE)	Coef.	(SE)
Constant	0.007	(0.002)	0.009	(0.003)
Δm_t	0.651	(0.119)	0.167	(0.387)
Δm_{t-1}	0.226	(0.128)	0.615	(0.320)
Δm_{t-2}	0.308	(0.148)	0.191	(0.251)
Δm_{t-3}	0.148	(0.182)	0.401	(0.341)
Δm_{t-4}	−0.240	(0.155)	−0.297	(0.240)
Δg_t	0.099	(0.031)	−0.190	(0.221)
Δg_{t-1}	0.026	(0.032)	0.058	(0.079)
Δg_{t-2}	0.005	(0.032)	0.049	(0.055)
Δg_{t-3}	−0.050	(0.032)	−0.025	(0.048)
Δg_{t-4}	−0.038	(0.031)	−0.033	(0.044)
R^2	0.531		0.053	
DW	1.90		1.91	
SE	0.0080		0.0113	

*Instruments are fitted values from OLS regressions of Δm_t and Δg_t on $\Delta m_{t-1},...,\Delta m_{t-4}$, $\Delta g_{t-1},...,\Delta g_{t-4}$, r_{t-1}, r_{t-2}, and a constant. The dependent variable in each case is Δy_t.

as a group with coefficients summing to 1.09, whereas the fiscal variables enter less strongly and their coefficients sum to only 0.04.[13]

In the second pair of numerical columns are IV estimates for the same period, with the instruments for Δm_t and Δg_t created by first-stage regressions of those variables on their lagged values Δm_{t-1}, Δg_{t-1}, ..., Δm_{t-4}, Δg_{t-4}, plus r_{t-1} and r_{t-2}, with r_t the 90-day treasury bill rate. Indentification is provided by the assumption that r_{t-1} and r_{t-2} affect policy instrument settings in period t. Because there is no strong sign of serially correlated disturbances, these estimates should be consistent for the parameters of (5) even in the presence of current-period responses of Δm_t and Δg_t to values of Δy_t or other endogenous variables. As is readily apparent, there are two major differences in these estimates as compared to OLS. First, the coefficients attached to current-period values of Δm_t and Δg_t are much smaller, with the latter turning negative. Second, the standard errors are much larger, indicating a substantial reduction in the reported accuracy of the coefficient estimators. In part, the latter is induced by lower overall explanatory power, but in part it is also due to the increased collinearity that arises when Δm_t and Δg_t are replaced by constructed variables that are primarily linear combinations of lagged Δm and Δg values.

It therefore appears from this experiment that the effects stressed by Goldfeld and Blinder may indeed be of quantitative importance. Yet even in these estimates it remains the case that the coefficients of

$\Delta m_t, \ldots, \Delta m_{t-4}$ sum to approximately 1.0, whereas those on $\Delta g_t, \ldots, \Delta g_{t-4}$ sum to approximately zero. (The numbers are 1.08 and -0.14, respectively.)[14]

Once it is recognized—as seems necessary—that policy instruments are set in response to current or recent conditions, then the motivation for using high unemployment values of fiscal variables is lessened or eliminated. Furthermore, it even becomes unclear why a distinction is drawn between "discretionary" changes in expenditures or taxes and automatic changes brought about as a result of the *built-in stabilizers*. It would be appropriate to distinguish empirically between automatic and nonautomatic instrument changes if there were theoretical reasons to believe that these would have different effects on nominal GNP, but the econometric reasons apparently motivating Andersen and Jordan (1968) do not seem applicable.[15] Consequently, it would appear that there remains room for an empirical study that emphasizes the endogenous-policy effects emphasized by Goldfeld and Blinder, and that also considers the impact on aggregate demand of tax changes brought about by the built-in stabilizers of the U.S. tax system. A major reason why such a study is still lacking is the difficulty in modeling policy behavior, together with the absence of genuine exogenous variables.

2.3 The Modigliani–Ando study

Let us now turn to the rather interesting experiment conducted by Modigliani and Ando (1976), who hypothesize that (even ignoring endogenous-policy issues) estimates of policy multipliers obtained by means of the St. Louis approach are extremely unreliable. In support of that hypothesis, Modigliani and Ando report that the St. Louis equation, when estimated using artificial data generated by simulations of the MPS model, provides very poor estimates of that model's *known* multipliers—estimates that are on the low side for fiscal multipliers and on the high side for monetary multipliers. Although this finding does not literally imply that the St. Louis estimates of the economy's multipliers are incorrect, it has been regarded by several reviewers[16] as tending to discredit the St. Louis procedure and, thus, its results.

Reflection suggests, however, that this conclusion may not be warranted: The reason for doubt involves the point made above—that there are virtually no macroeconomic variables that can appropriately be treated as exogenous. If that point is correct, then the Modigliani–Ando experiment will be misleading in the following way. Under the hypothesis at hand— that there are no exogenous variables—the MPS model (which treats a large number of variables as exogenous) incorrectly omits a large number of behavioral relationships analogous to (3). Therefore the "true" multiplier values for the MPS model reported by Modigliani and Ando correspond to the $\beta(L)$ and $\gamma(L)$ values in Eq. (2). But estimates of the MPS multipliers obtained by the St. Louis approach correspond to the $\beta'(L)$ and $\gamma'(L)$ coefficients in (5), with a_j values in (3) being whatever is implied by the historical values of the variables treated (incorrectly) as exogenous, the historical values of the policy instruments, and the simulated values of the model's endogenous variables. In other words, the comparison reported is between actual MPS values of the coefficients in (2) and estimated values of the coefficients in (5). Since these coefficients are truly different, under the hypothesis that there are no exogenous variables in reality, the discrepancy between estimated and true values does not indicate unreliability of the estimation procedure.[17] This argument, it should be said, seems to amount to an elaboration of the comment provided by Darby (1976).

2.4 Evidence from large models

One useful feature of the Meyer–Rasche survey is its compact tabulation of policy multipliers for real GNP implied by seven prominent macroeconometric models. Although there is considerable disagreement among the other models concerning the magnitudes of fiscal and monetary multipliers, the St. Louis results do depart significantly from the average values of the other models. The government spending multiplier after four quarters, for example, is 0.5 for the St. Louis model as compared with a mean of 2.17 for the BEA, Brookings, Michigan, DRI, MPS, and Wharton models. In the case of the monetary variable, the comparison is not straightforward, because the St. Louis multipliers pertain to an M1 variable, and the others pertain to unborrowed reserves. But the other-model average about four quarters is 3.0, so the St. Louis value of 4.4 is *much* greater in elasticity terms, the ratio of M1 to unborrowed reserves being about 10.

It will be noted that these multipliers are for *real* GNP, so their magnitudes depend upon the model's precise specifications of dynamic Phillips relationships. Since it is well known that there exist major disagreements over the proper specification of this relationship, it is, in principle, not surprising that the multipliers diverge. What one might hope for is some agreement concerning nominal GNP multipliers. That, in any event, is the topic under discussion in this paper—the relative impact of monetary and fiscal actions on aggregate *demand*.

But the foregoing statement applies only in principle. In fact, the predicted price level responses from any of the models in question are so slow that four-quarter multipliers are essentially the same both for nominal and real GNP. Thus we see that there is a considerable discrepancy between St. Louis and other-model responses to a monetary policy action, though less than in the case of a fiscal policy action.

Niehans (1978) and McNelis (1980) have suggested that the implications of non–St. Louis econometric models are actually much more "monetarist" than most observers have recognized. Their argument starts with the idea that the proper comparison of fiscal versus monetary policy effects requires that an unreversed $1 billion/year increase in government spending should be compared with a continuing sequence of $1 billion increases, one per year, in the high-powered money stock. And when this comparison is made, it is found that "for every model except BEA and Wharton III . . . the peak of the money multipliers must be many times as high as the peak of the hypothetical fiscal multipliers, a typical ratio being perhaps 15:1 . . . . The proposition that the quantity of money matters much more than the way it is created is evidently common to both" monetarist and nonmonetarist models (Niehans 1978, 253).

At first glance, this argument seems flawed. What is the point of comparing effects of changes in stock and flow variables? But then one realizes that it is entirely appropriate to compare an unreversed $1 billion change in expenditures financed by bond sales with a similar expenditure change financed by money issues—the bond or money issues going on period after period with total tax receipts unchanged. And, clearly, the second of these sequences is equivalent to the first plus a continuing sequence of open-market bond purchases. Thus the bond-financed expenditure increase and the sequence of open-market purchases are the two constituent parts of a money-financed expenditure increase. If the second constituent is much larger than the first, as Niehans and McNelis claim, then their comparison would be both sensible and justified.

Continuing to reflect reminds one, however, that the simulation experiments actually carried out in the large-scale models are ones that hold constant tax *rates*, not tax receipts. Thus, putative bond-financed expenditures and bond-financed money stock expansions are in fact tax financed to a considerable extent. This would tend, since the models are not Ricardian, to depress multiplier values. It is not obvious to me that this tends to bias the results in favor of either type of policy action, but it would be preferable to compare the effects of the following two experiments:

(i)   an unreversed expansion of government expenditures financed by bond sales, with unchanged tax-receipt and money-stock paths.

(ii) an unreversed expansion of government expenditures financed by (high-powered) money issue, with unchanged tax-receipt and bond-stock paths.

I would not be surprised if the outcome of such an experiment were to support the Niehans–McNelis position–which in turn supports that of St. Louis to a considerable extent–but as far as I can tell it has not yet been conducted.

2.5 Sims's VAR evidence

Before concluding this section, we should mention the argument recently advanced by Sims (1980, 1982) to the effect that the impact of monetary policy actions on GNP is extremely small. This argument stems from vector autoregression (VAR) results, obtained by Sims, that show that money-stock innovations[18] have very little explanatory power for U.S. postwar output when an interest rate is included among the VAR system's variables. These results have been interpreted as indicating that monetary policy actions have been an unimportant source of movements in real GNP–which would be, given the apparent slowness of price level responses, inconsistent with St. Louis-type results for nominal GNP as well. In a brief analytical note, however, I have shown that this conclusion is not implied by the empirical results in question (McCallum 1983). The point is that money-stock innovations do not necessarily reflect irregular components of monetary *policy*. Indeed, when the Fed uses an interest rate as its operating instrument–as it has during most of the postwar period–it is likely that its irregular actions will be better represented by a VAR system's interest rate innovations than by its money-stock innovations.[19] And in fact interest-rate innovations do contribute importantly to output movements in Sims's results. Thus, it cannot be concluded that the actions of the monetary authority are unimportant for the explanation of output and nominal GNP movements.[20]

3. Theoretical Issues

Let us begin the theoretical discussion by reviewing the effects of monetary and fiscal actions on aggregate demand in a *Ricardian* economy–that is one in which agents take account of the government budget restraint (GBR) in making savings–consumption decisions for an effectively infinite planning horizon.[21] Under such conditions the asset value of government bonds held by the public is offset by the present value of extra future taxes necessitated by the existence of these bonds, so the latter do not constitute wealth to the private sector as a whole. Thus a one-period tax reduction financed by bond sales has no effect on aggregate demand, for the implied increase in future taxes just offsets the effect on wealth of the reduction of current taxes. This Ricardian equivalence result, well known from the work of Barro (1974, 1984), provides the basis for a comparative analysis of monetary and fiscal policy effects.

The case of a tax reduction financed by *money* creation is quite different, for the asset value of the additional money is not offset by extra implied future taxes, of which there are none.[22] The added nominal wealth may be negated *in real terms* by inflation, but the latter comes about as the result of an upward shift in aggregate demand, which is precisely the effect being claimed. Thus, the fact that inflation may, for some purposes, be viewed as imposing a "tax" does not alter the validity of the statement beginning this paragraph; a money-financed tax cut increases nominal wealth and aggregate demand.

Consequently, since a money-financed tax cut (of, say, λ) and a bond-financed tax increase (of λ) are together equivalent to an open-market purchase, we see that an open-market purchase unambiguously increases aggregate demand (in a Ricardian economy).[23] This result clearly implies that an increase in government spending must have a larger stimulative effect on aggregate demand if it is money financed rather than bond financed, for the difference in the two actions is precisely an open-market purchase (or sequence of purchases if we are discussing an unreversed increase in government purchases).[24]

It remains to be considered whether a bond- (or tax-) financed increase in government purchases will have a nonzero effect on aggregate demand. Effects of both temporary and permanent changes in government spending in a Ricardian world have been analyzed, in nonmathematical but careful fashion, by Barro (1984, 309–312 and 316–320). In the case of a temporary increase there is an increase in output and in the real rate of interest. The latter translates, in the absence of inflation, into a rise in the nominal rate. For portfolio balance with a constant money stock, nominal income must then rise, if the income elasticity of real money demand is less than unity. To see this, let us write the money demand function as

$$m - p = \alpha_0 + \alpha_1 y - \alpha_2 r, \tag{6}$$

where m, p, and y are in logarithmic terms, r is the interest rate, and all parameters are positive. This equation may be rearranged to read

$$y + p = m - \alpha_0 + (1 - \alpha_1)y + \alpha_2 r, \tag{7}$$

so if $\alpha_1 < 1$ the increases in both y and r tend to increase $y + p$, the log of nominal income. In the case of a permanent increase in government spending, Barro's analysis leads to no chnage in r but, again, to an increase in y, so again (7) indicates a rise in $y + p$.[25] Thus we see that an increase in (real) government spending tends to induce an increase in aggregate demand.

In summary, a Ricardian analysis suggests that (i) open-market purchases are expansionary, so (ii) money-financed spending increases or tax cuts are more expansionary than bond-financed ones. Indeed, (iii) bond-financed tax cuts have no effect on aggregate demand, but (iv) bond-financed spending increases are expansionary.

Now it is, of course, not the case that Ricardian assumptions are literally satisfied by the U.S. economy. But the Ricardian model may nevertheless provide a useful first approximation to the workings of the economy, a fruitful starting point for thinking about the effects of policy actions. In particular, it would seem more appropriate to regard bonds as contributing to private wealth not at all, than to regard them as doing so fully. If each dollar of bonds functions macroeconomically as k dollars of net private wealth—which is the way Patinkin (1965, 289) puts it—then the value of k is (I would conjecture) much closer to 0.0 than to 1.0.[26]

The relevance of this observation is, of course, that most of the theoretical literature of monetary versus fiscal policy effects has presumed—usually without discussion—that bonds constitute wealth fully (i.e., that $k = 1.0$). Indeed, this literature abounds with paradoxical results that obtain in large part because of wealth effects due to ongoing expansion or contraction of government debt.[27] Another source of paradox in this literature—the exposition of which emphasizes the role of the GBR[28]—has been the practice of focusing on "long-run" effects, with the latter somewhat misleadingly defined so as to require a balanced budget. The inappropriateness of this terminology is emphasized by occasional statements concerning the comparative long-run effects of money- and bond-financed *deficit* spending.[29]

In any event there is one contention with which I want to take issue that appears in this literature: the notion that open-market purchases are contractionary or that, as Blinder and Solow (1976, 500) put it, "the long-run effect of government spending is greater when deficits are bond-financed than when they are money-financed."[30] The basis of this contention is, as explained in McCallum (1981, 136), that in models of the type now under discussion either the contention is true *or* the economy is dynamically unstable when deficits are bond financed (i.e., when paths of spending, the money stock, and income tax *rates* are determined exogenously so that the stock of bonds must adjust to satisfy the GBR). Then by assuming stability, the authors in question obtain the result. But, as is argued in detail in McCallum (1981, 136–137), the appropriate conclusion is rather that the economy is unstable[31] under these conditions, and open-market purchases are expansionary even according to the models and concepts in question.[32] That conclusion is in no way refuted by the observed stability of the U.S. economy, because neither the money stock nor taxes are in fact managed in the way assumed by the setup in which the analysis is conducted.

4. Conclusions

The substantive conclusions of the foregoing investigation/review are fairly easy to discern and are not very dramatic. The clearest is that an open-market increase in the money stock has a stimulative effect on aggregate demand—a conclusion that, in turn, implies that a money-financed increase in expenditures (or reduction in taxes) is more stimulative than a bond-financed increase. This conclusion is supported by empirical results obtained both from St. Louis-style estimates and from large-scale econometric models. Furthermore, the conclusion is also supported by theoretical analysis involving both Ricardian and non-Ricardian assumptions.

In the case of pure fiscal policy actions—that is, bond-financed tax cuts or bond-financed expenditure increases—the situation is not as clear. But theory suggests that the latter should be at least as stimulative as the former and most probably stimulative to a positive extent. The evidence on these points is mixed but is not obviously inconsistent with the theoretical predictions.

With respect to the textbook issue concerning the relative (per dollar) effect of pure monetary and fiscal actions, the evidence seems—in a rather disorderly way—to support the notion that a sequence of $\$\lambda$ open-market purchases, on each period, will be considerably more stimulative than a single but unreversed $\$\lambda$/period, bond-financed increase in expenditures.

It might be added, however, that it is unclear that any great importance attaches to this last issue, at least from a policy perspective, provided that each type of policy has nonnegligible effects. If the object of the debate is to determine whether monetary or fiscal variables would serve better as instruments to be manipulated for stabilization purposes, then attention should be focused on the relative *accuracy* of the effects rather than on the per dollar magnitudes. Adjustments in the instrument settings do not themselves involve costs, in terms of destroyed resources, as is implicitly suggested by the view that it is relative magnitudes that matter.[33] Nor is it entirely clear why, from a policy standpoint,[34] so much attention has been devoted to whether the *sum* of fiscal policy coefficients is zero when individual coefficients are significantly nonzero. Only a minor quibble[35] keeps me from sharing Fischer's (1976) view that "if fiscal policy had significant short-term effects . . . but no long-run effects it would be an ideal stabilization tool."

More generally, the essential issues concerning stabilization policy that continue to divide macroeconomists are those concerned with, first, the desirability of activist policy and, second, whether activist policy (if desirable) should be executed according to well-specified rules or in a period-by-period discretionary manner.[36,37] As various writers have noted,[38] neither of these issues is strongly dependent upon the outcome of the relative magnitudes question. That does not imply, however, that the monetary versus fiscal policy debate has been unenlightening. On the contrary, the various ins and outs of the discussion have served valuably to enhance knowledge and awareness of the central importance of monetary actions as determinants of nominal income. That contribution is easy to belittle or overlook, given today's wide acceptance of that importance. But the formation of today's views—that is, the dramatic change away from the situation described by Cagan—amounted to a major overhaul in the practice of macro and monetary economics, and this change was aided substantially by the monetary versus fiscal policy debate.

Notes

1. Another interesting sign of the items is provided by Michael Parkin's first notable publication (Lipsey and Parkin 1970), which centers on a "prototype model" of the wage and price inflation process. The model's two endogenous variables are the money wage and the price level; its exogenous variables are import prices, output/manhour, the unemployment rate, and a measure of trade union aggressiveness. Unless I am mistaken, there is no mention of "money" in the entire paper. This example will be appreciated most by those of us who know and admire Parkin's later work as a monetary economist.

2. The original paper was Andersen and Jordan (1968), soon followed by Andersen and Carlson (1970). Other notable items in the series include Carlson (1978), Hafer (1982), and Batten and Thornton (1983).

3. Friedman and Meiselman used M2 as their monetary variable and defined autonomous expenditures as "net private domestic investment plus the government deficit on income and product account plus the net foreign balance" (1963) 184). They also calculated partial correlations and devoted some attention to quarterly data.

4. An interesting predecessor of the Andersen–Jordan study, which probably influenced the latter, is Brunner and Balbach (1959).

5. Carlson (1978) indicates that the relative change specification passes, and the absolute change specification fails, tests for the absence of disturbance heteroskedasticity.

6. Or variables. My discussion proceeds as if only one such variable were omitted solely for convenience of exposition.

7. The impact of variables that follow smooth exponential trends is, of course, picked up by the constant term. This was noted (for linear trends) by Andersen and Jordan (1968).

8. That the disturbance in (5) is a complicated function of current and lagged values of the disturbance in (1) does not necessarily imply that the former is serially correlated, for the properties of the latter are unknown.

9. This point was made by Andersen and Jordan (1968), Darby (1976), and probably others. It will arise again in the discussion of the Modigliani–Ando (1976) results.

10. It is a Keynesian multiplier model.

11. Meyer and Rasche (1980, 59) conclude their discussion of this measurement issue as follows: "However, the modifications . . . have not generally resulted in dramatic changes in sample reduced-form equations."

12. Potential empirical importance is suggested by Modigliani and Ando (1976, 40–41).

13. Whether the magnitudes of these sums are important will be discussed in Section 4.

14. Similar conclusions obtain when once- and twice-lagged values of the unemployment rate for adult males are also used in the first-stage regressions, although in this case the results are closer to those obtained by OLS.

15. For a recent review of the theory of automatic stabilizers, see Christiano (1984).

16. These include Meyer and Rasche (1980, 62), Purvis (1980, 108–9), and McCallum (1978, 322).

17. Variants of this argument would appear to apply to the other Modigliani–Ando results.

18. A variable's innovation is its one-period ahead prediction error when the prediction is the orthogonal projection of the variable on all past values of the variables included in the system under consideration.

19. I do not mean to claim that interest-rate innovations actually reflect *only* policy surprises. They do in the formal model in McCallum (1983) but would not if the Fed's operating procedure were slightly different than that assumed. The main point of the demonstration is that it is unreasonable to use money-stock innovations as representative of monetary policy surprises.

20. This argument does not imply that interest rates are, in general, better "indicators" than money-stock growth rates of monetary policy impulses; the relations mentioned in the text hold only for innovations.

21. Also needed, of course, is the assumption that taxes are lump sum in nature—that is, have no major substitution effects. That finite-lived individuals may have effectively infinite planning horizons was shown by Barro (1974).

22. See Patinkin (1965, 289). The reason money is willingly held despite the absence of the interest payments is, of course, that it provides transaction-facilitating services to its holders.

23. An open-market purchase leaves fewer bonds outstanding and so requires smaller interest payments in the future by the government. Under Ricardian assumptions it does not matter whether this reduction in payments is accompanied by lower taxes or by bond growth.

24. That maintained deficits are possible under bond finance, as well as under money finance, is demonstrated in McCallum (1984a).

25. This type of result can be shown to hold in the Sidrauski-type version of the Ricardian model used by McCallum (1984a) as follows. As in Barro (1984), let the consumer obtain utility from government-provided services and express this by writing the within-period utility function for the representative household as $u(c_t + \alpha g_t, m_t)$ with $0 < \alpha < 1$. The budget constraint is not changed, so the household's optimality conditions remain (3)–(10) in McCallum (1984a, 128–129). Consider alternative steady states with zero inflation. Combining (4) and (5) then yields

$$\beta u_2(c + \alpha g,m) = (1 - \beta)u_1(c + \alpha g,m).$$

In this particular model an increase in g has no effect on the steady-state value of k (see p. 129), so $c + g$ is unaffected, and an increase in g lowers $z \equiv c + \alpha g$. From the equation above we have

$$\frac{dm}{dz} = \frac{u_{21} + \beta^{-1}(\beta-1)u_{11}}{u_{12}(1-\beta)\beta^{-1}-u_{22}}.$$

From the latter plus the conditions $u_{11} < 0$, $u_{22} < 0$, and $u_{12} > 0$, we find that $dm/dz > 0$. So real money balances fall with a reduction in z coming from an increase in g. But with a constant money stock, that implies an increase in the price level and thus in aggregate demand.

26. This condition does not require that individuals' planning horizons extend beyond their own lifetimes. I would also conjecture that analysis using the recently developed approach of Blanchard (1984) would support my main conclusions.

27. Some of the prominent items are included in volumes edited by Gordon (1974) and Stein (1976). Also influential were Christ (1968), Brunner and Meltzer (1972), and a series of papers by Blinder and Solow (1973, 1974, 1976). A recent review, which shares the criticized presumption of the items reviewed, is Mayer (1984).

28. It is worth noting that analysis that ignores the GBR is not thereby discredited, as long as it does not pretend that time paths of money, bonds, spending, and taxes can all be specified arbitrarily. An analysis that specifies paths for only three of these variables arbitrarily and ignores the fourth, may be perfectly logical as long as it does not require an infeasible path for the fourth variable—for example, a path along which the bond stock grows exponentially at a rate exceeding the growth rate of output by more than the rate of time preference (McCallum 1984a). Failing to keep track of the fourth variable may lead to errors if the model is non-Ricardian, because of induced shifts in behavioral relations. But if it is Ricardian and the fourth variable is bonds or tax receipts, then such shifts will not occur.

29. See, for example, Blinder and Solow (1976, 506).

30. Their contention is accepted by Mayer (1984).

31. In McCallum (1981) it is suggested that the dynamic instability in question can be avoided if the rate of output growth exceeds the after-tax real rate of return. But with an income tax, a maximizing analysis in a Ricardian model of the type used in McCallum (1984a) indicates that the steady-state, after-tax real rate of return will equal the rate of growth plus the rate of time preference. So the condition mentioned in my earlier paper as an escape from instability cannot hold in the vicinity of the steady state. I was thus wrong to quarrel, in my 1981 paper, with the first of the two "messages" suggested by Blinder and Solow (1976).

32. This conclusion seems to agree with that of Christ (1979, 533).

33. A similar point was mentioned by Meltzer (1969, 31) but only with respect to monetary instruments. Robert King has suggested to me that there may be resource costs associated with adjustments of tax schedules or government expenditures, that would tend to make money the better instrument.

34. The question of whether the cumulative effect of such actions is stimulative, contractionary, or neither may be of theoretical interest, since it bears on the appropriateness of competing theories. It is not the case, however, that a value of unity for the sum of the monetary policy coefficients is necessary for "long run"

monetary neutrality. For a recent discussion relating to that point, see McCallum (1984b).

35. The quibble is that zero effects after the first period, rather than zero long-run effects, would appear to be preferable.

36. The efficacy of various possible instruments and institutional arrangements is also of importance.

37. The advantage of rule-like behavior of monetary policy has been articulated by Barro and Gordon (1983).

38. Among these are Sargent (1976), Modigliani (1977), and McCallum (1978).

References

Ackley, Gardner. 1961. *Macroeconomic Theory*. New York: Macmillan.

Andersen, Leonall C., and Jerry L. Jordan. 1968. Monetary and fiscal actions: A test of their relative importance in economic stabilization. *Federal Reserve Bank of St. Louis Review* 50: 11–24.

Andersen, Leonall C., and Keith M. Carlson. 1970. A monetarist model for economic stabilization. *Federal Reserve Bank of St. Louis Review* 52: 7–25.

Ando, Albert, and Franco Modigliani. 1965. The relative stability of monetary velocity and the investment multiplier. *American Economic Review* 50: 693–728.

Barro, Robert J. 1974. Are government bonds net wealth? *Journal of Political Economy* 82: 1095–1117.

_____ 1984. *Macroeconomics*. New York: Wiley.

Barro, Robert J., and David B. Gordon. 1983. A positive theory of monetary policy in a natural rate model. *Journal of Political Economy* 91: 589–610.

Batten, Dallas S., and Daniel L. Thornton. 1983. Polynomial distributed lags and the St. Louis equation. *Federal Reserve Bank of St. Louis Review* 65: 13–25.

Blanchard, Olivier J. 1984. Debt, deficits, and finite horizons. NBER Working Paper No. 1389.

Blinder, Alan S., and Robert M. Solow. 1973. Does fiscal policy still matter? *Journal of Public Economics* 2: 319–37.

_____ 1974. Analytical foundations of fiscal policy. In *The Economics of Public Finance*. Washington: Brookings Institution.

_____ 1976. Does fiscal policy still matter? A reply. *Journal of Monetary Economics* 2: 501–10.

Brunner, Karl, and Anatol B. Balbach. 1959. An evaluation of two types of monetary theories. In *Proceedings of the 34th Annual Conference of the Western Economic Association*.

Brunner, Karl, and Allan H. Meltzer. 1972. Money, debt, and economic activity. *Journal of Political Economy* 80: 951–77.

Cagan, Phillip. 1978. Monetarism in historical perspective. In *The Structure of Monetarism*, ed. T. Mayer. New York: Norton.

Carlson, Keith M. 1978. Does the St. Louis equation now believe in fiscal policy? *Federal Bank of St. Louis Review* 60: 13–19

Christ, Carl F. 1968. A simple macroeconomic model with a government budget restraint. *Journal of Political Economy* 76: 53–67.

_____ 1979. On fiscal and monetary policies and the government budget restraint. *American Economic Review* 69: 526-38.

Christiano, Lawrence J. 1984. A reexamination of the theory of automatic stabilizers. In *Carnegie–Rochester Conference Series on Public Policy*, Vol. 20, 147–206.

Corrigan, E. Gerald. 1970. The Measurement and importance of fiscal policy changes. *Federal Reserve Bank of New York Monthly Review* 52: 133–45.

Darby, Michael. 1976. Comments. In *Monetarism*, ed. J. L. Stein. Amsterdam: North-Holland.

De Prano, Michael, and Thomas Mayer. 1965. Tests of the relative importance of autonomous expenditures and money. *America Economic Review* 55: 729–52.

Fischer, Stanley. 1976. Comments. In *Monetarism*, ed. J. L. Stein. Amsterdam: North-Holland.

Friedman, Benjamin M. 1977. Even the St. Louis model now believes in fiscal policy. *Journal of Money, Credit, and Banking* 9: 365–67.

_____ 1984. Money, credit, and interest rates in the business cycle. NBER Working Paper No. 1482.

Friedman, Milton, and David Meiselman. 1963. The relative stability of monetary velocity and the investment multiplier in the United States, 1897–1958. In *Stabilization Policies*. Englewood Cliffs: Prentice-Hall.

Goldfeld, Stephen M., and Alan S. Blinder. 1972. Some implications of endogenous stabilization policy. *Brookings Papers on Economic Activity* No. 3: 585–640.

Gordon, Robert A., and Lawrence Klein, eds. 1965. *Readings in Business Cycles*. Homewood, Il.: Richard D. Irwin.

Gordon, Robert J., ed. 1974. *Milton Friedman's Monetary Framework*. Chicago: University of Chicago Press.

Gordon, Robert J., and Stephen King. 1982. The output costs of disinflation in traditional and vector autoregression models. *Brookings Papers on Economic Activity* No. 1: 205–42.

Hafer, R. W. 1982. The role of fiscal policy in the St. Louis equation. *Federal Reserve Bank of St. Louis Review* 59: 17–22.

Hester, Donald D. 1964. Keynes and the quantity theory: A comment on the Friedman–Meiselman CMC paper. *Review of Economics and Statistics* 46: 364–77.

Lipsey, Richard G., and J. M. Parkin. 1970. Incomes policy: A reappraisal. *Economica* 37: 115–38.

Litterman, Robert. 1982. Specifying vector autoregressions for macroeconomic forecasting. Working Paper No. 208, Federal Reserve Bank of Minneapolis.

Lucas, Robert E., Jr. 1976. Econometric policy evaluation: A critique. In *Carnegie–Rochester Conference Series in Public Policy*, Vol. 1, K. Brunner and A. H. Meltzer, eds. Amsterdam: North-Holland.

Mayer, Thomas. 1984. The government budget constraint and standard macrotheory. *Journal of Monetary Economics* 13: 371–79.

McCallum, Bennett T. 1981. Monetarist principles and the money stock growth rule. *American Economic Review* 71: 134–38.

_____ 1983. A reconsideration of Sims's evidence concerning monetarism. *Economics Letters* 13: 167–71.

_____ 1984a. Are bond-financed deficits inflationary? A Ricardian Analysis. *Journal of Political Economy* 92: 123–35.

_____ 1984b. On low-frequency estimates of long-run relationships in macroeconomics. *Journal of Monetary Economics* 14: 3–14.

_____ 1978. Book review. *Journal of Monetary Economics* 4: 321–24.

McNelis, Paul D. 1980. Irrepressible monetarists conclusions from a non-monetarist model. *Journal of Monetary Economics* 6: 121–27.

Meltzer, Allan H. 1969. Money, intermediation, and growth. *Journal of Economic Literature* 7: 27–57.

Meyer, Lawrence H., and Robert H. Rasche. 1980. Empirical evidence on the effects of stabilization policy. In *Stabilization Policies: Lessons from the '70s and Implications for the '80s.* Center for the Study of American Business.

Modigliani, Franco. 1977. Monetarist controversy or, should we forsake stabilization policies? *American Economic Review* 67: 1–19.

Modigliani, Franco, and Albert Ando. 1976. Impacts of fiscal actions on aggregate income and the monetarist controversy: Theory and evidence. In *Monetarism*, ed. J. L. Stein. Amsterdam: North-Holland.

Neihans, Jurg. 1978. *The Theory of Money.* Balitmore: Johns Hopkins Press.

Patinkin, Don. 1965. *Money, Interest, and Prices.* 2d ed. New York: Harper and Row.

Purvis, Douglas D. 1980. Monetarism: A review. *Canadian Journal of Economics* 13: 96–122.

Sargent, Thomas J. 1976. A classical macroeconometric model for the United States. *Journal of Political Economy* 84: 207–38.

Sims, Christopher A. 1980. Comparison of interwar and postwar business cycles: Monetarism reconsidererd. *American Economic Review* 70: 250–57.

———— 1982. Policy analysis with econometric models. *Brookings Papers on Economic Activity* No. 1: 107–52.

Stein, Jerome L., ed. *Monetarism.* Amsterdam: North-Holland.

Webb, Roy H. 1984. Vector autoregressions as a tool for forecast evaluation. *Federal Reserve Bank of Richmond Economic Review* 70: 3–11.

Part II

THE STATE OF
FISCAL POLICY THEORY

3

Fiscal Policy in Macro Theory:
A Survey and Evaluation

Karl Brunner
UNIVERSITY OF ROCHESTER

1. Background

Almost twenty years ago the "fiscalist issue" emerged as a major focus on macroeconomic debates. Milton Friedman and David Meiselman initiated the discussion with an article eventually published in the volumes of the "Monetary Commission." The debate was subsequently joined in the middle 1960s by Albert Ando, Michael De Prano, Donald Hester, Thomas Mayer, and Franco Modigliani. Jerry Jordan and Leonall Andersen, with other members of the research staff at the Federal Reserve Bank of St. Louis and their critics, continued the discussion toward the end of the 1960s into the early years of the 1970s.

Another round of discussions followed in the first half of the 1970s. The focus had somewhat changed, however. The Keynesian side acknowledged real effects of monetary influences, and the monetarists participating in the discussion recognized temporary real effects and permanent nominal effects of fiscal policy. Starting from this position, the contribution by Carl Christ (1968), Blinder and Solow (1974), Brunner (1976), and Brunner and Meltzer (1972a, 1972b, 1976) addressed mainly the feedback via the asset markets resulting from prevailing budgetary policies. This work reemphasized the idea of a "crowding out" of private capital formation associated with the financing of a budget deficit.

The appearance of "rational expectations" with the seminal work of Robert Barro, Robert Lucas, and Thomas Sargent modified our approach to monetary processes. It affected also the analysis of fiscal policy. The basic thrust provided by the prevailing formation of "rational expectations" encouraged the revival of an idea originally pondered by Ricardo. Rational expectations of agents expressing concern for future generations destroys the significance of financial decisions in the budget process. The financing of current expenditures with tax revenues or the sale of bonds yields the same results under the circumstances. Deficit finance determines future tax liabilities with a present value just matching the tax revenues currently suspended. Wealth, position, and opportunities of agents remain unchanged. Deficit finance affects, therefore, neither interest rates nor aggregate demand for output. This aspect of fiscal policy thus offers no wedge for influencing the aggregate evolution of the economy. This result contrasts both with Keynesian and inherited monetarist analysis. The ensuing discussions, however, uncovered processes linking tax policies (even lump sum policies) with real effects operating independently of direct portfolio and asset market effects. These processes are centered on intergenerational wealth transfers associated with debt and tax policies. The macroeconomic role of tax policies depends ultimately, so it appears, on the assumption of "intergenerational self-interest" or on specific risks and uncertainties.

An important role of tax policies apparently survives the emergence of rational expectations and so does a role for expenditure policies. Total expenditures and their structure still affect, in the context of this neoclassic analysis, consumption, investment, aggregate real demand for output, the supply of output, and real rates of interest. But the detailed nature of the mechanism differs radically from the Keynesian story. The government sector operates essentially as a production process absorbing products from the private sector as an input to produce an output. This output either competes with private consumption or contributes to the private sector's production process. This approach was originally suggested by Martin Bailey (1971) but disregarded by aggregate analysis. Both Keynesian and monetarist arguments treated "government" as a sinkhole swallowing a portion of private sector output. The emphasis on "government" as a production process operating with distortionary taxes changes the macroeconomic focus of fiscal policy in important ways.

The momentum of academic discussions substantially changed in retrospect the range of issues surrounding fiscal policy. The analytic evolutions and the resulting discussions modified many questions and emphasized new dimensions. Academic discussions were also influenced in recent years by political events and discussions in the public arena. The emergence of a comparatively large and possibly "permanent" deficit in the Federal budget motivated another round of discussions. There appeared voices claiming that such deficits produce, in contrast to Keynesian arguments, *negative* short-run effects on output. Others emphasized the long-run effects on normal growth. Many concentrated on linking high interest rates with the prevailing large deficit. The inflationary significance of the deficit was also considered. Some arguments seem to recognize a direct link between deficits and inflation. More carefully developed arguments emphasize the longer-run effect of persistent deficits on monetary policy. It would appear that an anti-inflationary policy pursued in the context of a permanent deficit cannot persist. Fiscal policy appears under the circumstances as the longer-run determinant of monetary policy and a crucial characteristic of the ultimately prevailing monetary regime. It follows that no reliable change in monetary regime is really feasible without an associated change in the long-run fiscal regime. This argument introduced a new focus and attention to fiscal policy.

The evolution of questions, issues, and analysis over the past nineteen years since the "war between the radio stations" (FM, AM, DM) in the *American Economic Review* (1965) justified in the judgment of the Conference organizers, and also in my judgment, an appraisal of our intellectual positions. My paper is addressed to this task. It offers essentially a survey over major strands of the discussion evolving over the past twenty years. This survey remains somewhat selective even within its confined range of macroeconomic issues. Neither does it cultivate a "neutral" account. It involves interpretations and evaluations referring to aspects of arguments advanced or to dimensions of the analysis that require more attention.

The first section covers the fiscalist–monetarist debate of the late sixties and early seventies. It evaluates the empirical work bearing on the central questions addressed at the time. The following section attends to the range of issues raised by the neoclassical cum rational expectations approach. Section 4 examines a number of problems recently associated with transitory and permanent deficits. The last section assesses the consequences of our intellectual position with respect to fiscal policy-making and the choice of fiscal regime.

2. The Fiscalist Issue

2.1. The fiscalist–monetarist debate

2.1.a. The evolving theme. The debate emerged gradually in the late 1950s and was fully focused at the time of the conference on monetary theory organized by the National Bureau of Economic Research in Pittsburgh (1963). The intellectual state was conditioned at the time by the critical response of an increasing number of economists to the prevailing Keynesian analysis of fiscal and monetary policy. The core of Keynes's *General Theory* presents a real theory of a low-level output trap. It is supplemented by a real theory of business cycles. The central theme emphasizes the operation of two fundamental failures embedded in economic organizations relying on markets for the social coordination of activities. These market failures center on the stock market, as a guide for investment activities, and the labor market. They severely damage the ability of a market system to function as an instrument of social coordination. The peculiar characteristics of the stock market shape, so the story goes, a price behavior randomly related to the social function of rational resource allocation. These characteristics also suspend a reliable feedback from the saving–consumption nexus to an investment decision. Persistent mass unemployment suggested, moreover, to Keynes that potentially beneficial transactions remained suspended. Such potentialities are expressed by an excess of the labor suppliers' marginal utility of the wage product over the marginal disutility of labor. The market process apparently fails to provide a sufficient range of coordinating mechanisms.

These basic failures embedded in the structure of the economic process could not be offset by increased wage flexibility or monetary manipulations. Such endeavors would produce, at most, temporary deviations from the low-level output trap (Meltzer 1981). A more powerful instrument was required to move the economy out of such doldrums and push it nearer to full employment. Fiscal policy seemed to offer the instrumental opportunities needed for Keynes's purpose. The underlying analysis suggested that fiscal policy could be shaped to influence directly aggregate expenditures and to affect indirectly, via the multiplier, the level of consumption expenditures and total output and employment.

The message infiltrated the profession with some variations on the theme. Alvin Hansen's secular stagnation centered on the basic real phenomenon subsequently formalized by the "Keynesian cross." This formulation reenforced the "fiscalist thesis" emerging from the Keynesian analysis, a thesis that attributed dominant positive and normative significance to fiscal policy as an instrument conditioning the level of output and employment. Sir John Hicks's reinterpretation in terms of the IS/LM ("islamic") paradigm complicated the pattern somewhat with its inclusion of a feedback via asset markets and portfolio adjustments. But the assumption of accommodating monetary policy or the prevailing view attributing low-interest elasticity to aggregate demand and high-interest elasticity to money demand yielded a close approximation to the implications of the "Keynesian cross." The professional literature of the late forties and fifties reveals this state very clearly. The article on monetary policy by Seltzer (1945) in the late 1940s effectively reflects the dominant intellectual mood. The book *Policies to Combat Depressions* (1956) based on a conference organized by the National Bureau of Economic Research expresses the basic theme. It concentrated fully and only on fiscal policy. The slowly evolving flood of textbooks conveyed the same message and so did, to mention another example, Tinbergen's book *On the Theory of Economic Policy* (1952.)

The existing professional state must be clearly perceived in order to understand the subsequent intellectual developments. Doubts and reservations bearing on the central underlying theme of market failure never vanished entirely. The victorious sweep of the fiscalist thesis did not silence some expressions of doubt. Clark Warburton pursued the classic program of monetary analysis, offering a substantive alternative to the Keynesian vision. Milton Friedman (1952) reenforced the questioning with an examination of the comparative role of government expenditures and monetary movements in three wartime experiences. The classic research program rejected the market-failure approach introduced by Keynes as a serious misinterpretation of market economics and of specific events observed in the 1930s. Substantial doubts about the role assigned to fiscal policy by the Keynesian position was unavoidable under the circumstances. The evolution of monetarist ideas thus continues essentially a classical program. These ideas reject the dominance of fiscal policy as a determinant of both short- and long-run, aggregate, nominal or real demands. At least some strands of the analysis acknowledge an effect of fiscal policy on short- and long-term *nominal* demands, and a short-term effect on real demand for output, but they deny any effect on long-term aggregate real demand. However, all strands attribute to monetary shocks substantial short- and long-term nominal effects and a definite short-term real effect. This basic position was, however, sharpened with a specific "impulse hypothesis" incorporated into monetarist analysis. This position reversed the Keynesian thesis and assigned a comparatively dominant role to monetary impulses within the general pattern described above. This thesis of a comparative dominance was not advanced as an "ontological proposition." It was interpreted to reflect simultaneously the response characteristics of the economic mechanism and the historical circumstances expressed by the relative magnitude and variability of fiscal and monetary impulses. The dominant impulse hypothesis maintained by the monetarist was thus quite sensitively dependent on the choice of financial regime.

2.1.b. The empirical work. The professional state characterizing the earlier postwar period outlined in the previous paragraph needs to be fully appreciated in order to assess the empirical work initiated in the late 1950s by Milton Friedman and David Meiselman. This article motivated critical responses by Donald Hester (1964), Ando and Modigliani (1965), and De Prano and Mayer (1965). Another round of empirical discussion was unleashed by Leonall Andersen and Jerry Jordan (1968) with an article in the *Review* published by the Federal Reserve Bank of St. Louis. Other members (Michael Keran and Keith Carlson) of the St. Louis Fed's staff extended the discussion and so did Keynesian critics from the Board's staff in Washington (DeLeeuw and Kalchbrenner 1969) and the Brookings Institution (Goldfeld and Blinder 1972).

Harry Johnson (1971) asserted in the early 1970s that the empirical discussion of the 1960s was fundamentally flawed and methodologically inadequate. Tobin (1981) recently repeated Johnson's assessment. The two authors thus convey an impression that little, if anything at all, can be learned from the first round of discussion about the role and significance of fiscal policy. Neither one of the authors, however, provides any references or offers any arguments or clues supporting their contention. The methodological objections raised at the time by Keynesians were apparently accepted at face value without further examination. It is noteworthy, therefore, that Keynesian critics justified their rather categorically formulated conclusions in terms of the same methodological procedure. An array of objections advanced with a categorical import frequently involved, moreover, nothing beyond invocations of possibly alternative, but unassessed, hypotheses. A retrospective appraisal from the vantage point of our current state of discussion may be useful for our purposes.

Consider first the basic purpose of the empirical work. It was addressed to a preliminary assessment of a wide and influential class of microeconomic hypotheses. An array of formulations filling textbooks and conveyed to the academic world with a sense of empirical relevance implied the dominant significance of fiscal policy and the irrelevance of monetary policy in shaping the evolution of output and nominal magnitudes. These implications were also mirrored by many policy statements supplied to the public arena. These broad statements about the nature of the economic process were the subject of a first round of searching investigation.

The examination, guided by the dominant underlying theme, essentially addressed a basic *class* of Keynesian theories. The class was determined by the specification of the income variable y, the autonomous expenditure variable A, and the linearity constraint. These specifications yielded the induced magnitude defined by $I = Y - A$ and the reduced forms $Y = \alpha + \beta A + \epsilon$ or $I = \gamma + \delta A + \nu$. A wide range of specific theories formulated with any given definition of Y and A yields the specific reduced forms. Changes in the definition of Y and A modify the relevant class under consideration. The dependence of the definition of I on the definitions of Y and A is crucial in this context. This requirement was occasionally violated by some authors. This basic class was contrasted with a "quantity-theory" of the form $Y = a + bM + \mu$ or $I = c + dM + w$. The "simple" K-class implies that β and δ are significantly positive, whereas b and d are zero. The "simple" version of the quantity-theory asserts the opposite.

The investigation extended beyond the basic class of income–expenditure theories. They included classes defined by the reduced forms $Y = \alpha + \beta A + \gamma M + \epsilon$ or $I = a + bA + cM + \mu$. These formulations subsume all standard versions constructed in accordance with the "islamic" paradigm. The underlying theme to be assessed implies that β dominates γ (or b dominates c) in significance.

The empirical assessment exploited both versions of the reduced form. The I-form offered a useful check on the Y-form. The latter produces a biased estimate of the A-coefficient due to the implicit correlations between Y and A, which would yield an apparently significant coefficient estimate for A even in the absence of any relevant systematic connection between I and A.

A remarkable fact emerged once the investigation was under way. We seemed to have been conditioned to assume that we understood what Keynesian theory meant. But such understanding required that the profession agree on the specification of autonomous expenditures. The investigations, however, revealed a remarkable disarray and confusion. The critical comments advanced by Friedman and Meiselman (1965, 73) in this respect are still worth noting today:

> We and our critics all used the same measures (for the money stock) without much ado. The contrast with 'autonomous expenditures' could hardly be sharper. Among us, we have produced more measures than there are critics. We settled on one; AM on a different one, which is the sum of two separable components; DM, after running 'basic tests ... on 20 different, but not unreasonable, definitions of autonomous expenditures' settle on two, but also carry two others along for the ride; Hester came up with four measures that only partly overlap the others. And all of us harbor serious doubts about the measures we settled on. However useful 'autonomous expenditures' may be as a theoretical construct, it is still far from having any generally accepted empirical counterpart.

Another passage in Friedman and Meiselman's comments also deserves our current attention. It cautions against the potential evaluation of Keynesian theory by choosing larger portions of Y and A:

> By our model, we in effect treated the income–expenditure theory as saying: if you know from other sources what is going to happen to roughly one-tenth of Y or N, then the multiplier analysis will tell you (or give you an estimate of) what will happen to the other nine-tenths. AM converts the model into one that says: if you know from other sources what is going to happen to nearly half of Y or over one-third of N, then the multiplier analysis will tell you what will happen to the other half of Y or two-thirds of N. DM's two models treat only slightly less of total income as autonomous. If AM and DM were to continue along this line of 'improving' the

model by having it predict a smaller and smaller percentage of income more and more accurately they would soon arrive at the point where it is predicting nothing—perfectly! In the old saw, with such friends, the income–expenditure theory hardly needs any enemies.

These issues found little attention at the time. They did reveal, however, that the sweep of Keynesian ideas, in spite of a vast literature and influential textbooks, had not been translated into a useful empirical theory. The strong assertions conveyed by the basic core of the income–expenditure approach, which frequently spilled over into categorical policy statements, were thus shown to have little substantive foundation.

2.1.c. The nature of objections and critique. An evaluation of the first-round discussion especially needs to consider the major objections advanced that possibly influenced Johnson's judgment, which was repeated by Tobin. Ando and Modigliani (1965), for instance, objected vehemently against the "single equation–single variable approach." They also criticized the use of "simple models" in lieu of "sophisticated models." Ando and Modigliani emphasized, in particular, at a later round of discussions that the regressions applied in the investigations under consideration were demonstrably inadequate to assess fiscalist propositions on the basis of observations controlled by a world conforming to a specific, large, econometric model (1976). Closely associated with these points was the accusation (or condemnation) that the procedure chosen reflected a "reduced form methodological commitment." This "simplistic" commitment was juxtaposed to the "sophistication" of a "structural" model. Authors were also inclined to criticize on grounds of "grievous misspecification." Ando and Modigliani, moreover, declared categorically that the examinations executed by Friedman and Meiselman are "basically irrelevant for the purpose of assessing the *empirical* uselessness of the income–expenditure framework." Disputes arose over the choice of exogenous variables. The other party's choices were naturally wrong, most particularly if one's own selection yielded approximately the desired estimate. Lastly, one author (Hester) asserted that "theory or intuition" was necessary to specify (correctly?) "the components of autonomous expenditures." This argument could, of course, be extended to the choice of exogenous variables.

These objections involve two important issues and reflect the confusions frequently emerging in the interpretation of the profession's empirical work. The first issue addressed by the critique emphasizes the "reduced form methodology," the "single-equation–single-variable" fallacy, or the propensity for simple, in lieu of, (more realistic?) "sophisticated" models. These objections essentially fail to recognize the rather specific and limited purpose of the investigations. This failure is especially visible in the quote drawn from the comments made by Ando and Modigliani. The "battery of tests" undertaken by Friedman and Meiselman and also the subsequent work contributed by the staff of the Federal Reserve Bank of St. Louis were not immediately directed to an assessment of the income–expenditure *framework*. A direct assessment of such a framework is logically impossible. Such assessments pertain to specific hypotheses or classes of hypotheses formulated in accordance with general criteria characterizing the framework. An assessment of the framework emerges ultimately from the cognitive fate of the hypotheses it generates. It would thus be clearly understood that none of the critical investigations was addressed to the framework. Previous passages emphasized that the assessment was directed at *particular classes* of hypotheses yielding strong propositions about the comparative significance of autonomous expenditures and at least potentially about fiscal policy. And once more, the prevalent intellectual state with its underlying theme fully justified this limited purpose—that is, limited relative to the general framework and its possible translation into classes of hypotheses.

The other three objections associated with the first issue involve different aspects or verbalizations of the same problem. The attribution of a methodological legislation insisting, as a matter of principle, on a reduced-form procedure reflects a pervasive misunderstanding about the logic of the procedure characterized above. The statements under examination pertaining to relative dominance of A do not bear *specifically* on any *particular* structure; that is, they do not characterize or single out in a detailed fashion a particular hypothesis. They consistently describe a whole class of hypotheses and actually pertain to *properties of the class*. The most efficient procedure, under the circumstances, for systematic assessment of such statements uses the reduced form as a test statement. The properties of the reduced form reflect the properties of the class of hypotheses under examination. Structural estimation of a single member of the class is inefficient and essentially uninformative for the purpose. No methodological legislation is thus involved.

The use of a single equation with a single independent variable should now be clear. It was the appropriate choice for an assessment of the core class. It did not represent a single equation *model* or a disposition to favor simple, as against sophistical, models. The "single equation with single variable" was the appropriate choice for an evaluation of a class of hypotheses seriously presented in textbooks and class teachings. The objection thus either misses the point or really tells us that all the chapters and classes elaborating the Keynesian cross or widely used versions of the "islamic" framework should be clearly labeled as irrelevant pastimes without any use for the justificiation of any policy statements. This would also involve a major separation from Keynes, Hansen, and an influential literature controlling undergraduate teaching during the 1950s and in our hinterlands still today.

A second issue embedded in the discussion bears on a pervasive confusion between logical issues and psychological effects. Our discussions frequently suffer under a disposition to *reject* an argument or hypothesis simply on the grounds that one is capable of formulating an alternative. Such ability offers, of course, no information about the cognitive status of the hypothesis under consideration. Objections adducing "misspecifications" are thus, by themselves, an empty gesture. They may be interpreted, however, as defining implicitly a program of further research. But the formulation of such a program possesses, by itself, no evidential value with respect to the initial hypothesis.

Some authors found that Friedman and Meiselman or Andersen and Jordan had committed some serious misspecifications. Ando and Modigliani developed, in particular, a "more sophisticated model" within the general "income–expenditure framework." They concluded from this construction that the evaluations made by Friedman and Meiselman were useless and irrelevant. We note first that the "laborious battery of tests" executed by Friedman and Meiselman and others is indeed irrelevant with respect to a wide class of hypotheses subsumable under the general income–expenditure paradigm. This critique would be properly addressed to *general* conclusions about the role of fiscal policy drawn from the empirical work actually executed. Friedman and Meiselman and Andersen and Jordan carefully avoided such sweeping conclusions. Their evaluations were made relative to a specific class of "Keynesian-type" models and their significance is conditioned by this context. The evaluations would still be correct but irrelevant and useless if the class of hypotheses under consideration was demonstrably neglected, disregarded, and without any influence on the profession's policy thinking. But the latter condition hardly describes the professional situation of the earlier postwar period.

Hester's argument pertaining to the choice of autonomous magnitudes deserved special attention in this context: he suggested that theory or intuition determine this choice. But this choice determines the precise nature of the empirical theory. There exists no such theory involving a definite empirical context before this choice is made. The notion of a "theory" guiding the choice alluded to by Hester refers at best to *formal* structure linking variables with generic names. The admissible range of semantic rules connecting variables via measurement procedures with observations still includes many diverse possibilities. Whatever a priori notions of "preempirical theory" or intuition we exploit for the specification of crucial magnitudes yield, however, no evidence of the empirical validity of the choice is made. Neither Hester's notion of a "theory" nor any intuition can judge the empirically relevant choices. The suggestion fundamentally misconceives the nature of scientific procedures and confuses the context of search for an hypothesis with the context of evaluation on the basis of critical observation.

2.1.d. The exogeneity issue. Hester's issue naturally generalizes to the specification of exogenous variables. Objections addressed to the selection or construction of exogenous magnitudes form a standard procedure of mutual criticism. But once again the execution of a set of regressions with more "desirable" coefficient patterns based on alternative choices of exogenous variables expresses a rival hypothesis but offers per se no relevant evidence discriminating between the alternative hypotheses. Reliance on the correlation coefficient must be carefully examined in these matters. Such reliance is quite appropriate for the evaluation of the core class addressed by Friedman and Meiselman. The hypothesis of comparative dominance implies systematic differences among correlation coefficients. We note in contrast that the eventual observation of higher correlation under *alternative* choices of monetary and fiscal variables possesses no evidential value discriminating between the selections. Such value can only exist relative to a specified class of hypotheses that *implies* statements about correlation patterns. This would require restriction on all the parameters, including a full description of stochastic properties under the alternative definitions. The observation of a comparatively high sample correlation and more "desirable" coefficient patterns under alternative exogeneity specifications in the absence of an initially formulated hypothesis therefore contains no discriminating cognitive significance. It forms at best the initial step in the formulation of an hypothesis still to be subsequently assessed against new data.

The exogeneity issue was further elaborated by Stephen M. Goldfeld and Alan S. Blinder (1972). The two authors explored in great and careful detail the implications of endogenous stabilization actions bearing on coefficient estimations in reduced forms. Their investigation is anchored by the reduced-form regressions used by Andersen and Jordan and expressed by Eq. (1). The symbols F and M refer to fiscal and monetary

$$y = k + \alpha F + \beta M + \epsilon \qquad (1)$$

variables, and ϵ is a random term. It is, of course, well known that any correlation between F and M and ϵ as a result of an endogenous policy regime produces biased and inconsistent estimators of α and β. Goldfeld and Blinder pursue the matter well beyond this general statement and impose some structure on the nature of the correlations. This structure reflects a variety of assumptions about the nature of endogenous stabilization policies. The endogenous policy variables can be represented as a sum of a nonstochastic magnitude, which can be neglected for our purposes, and a stochastic term

$$F = \frac{\epsilon_F}{\alpha} \ , \ M = \frac{\epsilon_M}{\beta},$$

where $\epsilon_F = \epsilon + u_F$, $\epsilon_M = \epsilon + u_m$, the variance of ϵ is σ^2, the variance of u_F is $\gamma^2\sigma^2$ and the variance of u_M is $\delta^2\sigma^2$. The u-terms reflect the forecasting ability of fiscal and monetary authorities exercised in the context of their stabilizing endeavors. The parameters γ and δ represent the authorities' forecasting ability. Lower values of γ and δ mean higher forecasting quality. Similar or coordinated forecasting may produce a correlation ρ between u_F and u_M. These assumptions imply the following probability limit for the ratios $\hat{\alpha}/\alpha$ and $\hat{\beta}/\beta$ of OLS estimates of the reduced form (1) to the true parameters

$$\frac{\hat{\alpha}}{\alpha} = 1 + \frac{\delta(\rho\alpha - \delta)}{\Delta}, \qquad \frac{\hat{\beta}}{\beta} = 1 + \frac{\gamma(\rho\delta - \gamma)}{\Delta},$$

$$\Delta = \gamma^2 + \delta^2 - \alpha\rho\gamma\delta + \gamma^2\delta^2(1 - \rho^2) > 0.$$

The three forecasting parameters associated with endogenous policy reactions clearly determine the outcome. Almost any combination of biases can be produced by shifting patterns of ρ, γ, and δ. With $\rho = 0$, δ large, and γ small, fiscal policy may appear to be insignificant in reduced-form regressions of Eq. (1). An excellent stabilization record of the fiscal authorities supplemented with a poor record of monetary authorities could explain the Andersen–Jordan results even against the background of a substantial α-coefficient.

The authors' general result is confirmed by elaborations of the argument. These elaborations include erroneous assumptions about the multipliers made by the authorities and lagged policy responses to serially correlated ϵ-disturbances. They extend to the case of "policy interaction" where one authority's response takes into account the other agency's behavior. The argument also covers a more general model with exogenous variables added to Eq. (1). All these cases enlarge the range for potential bias beyond the initial parameters ρ, γ, δ.

Goldfeld and Blinder supplement their analytic investigation of statistical implications associated with endogenous policy responses with a Monte Carlo study. They use an econometric model originally published by Moroney and Mason to generate data sets on the variables incorporated. These data sets were applied to structural and reduced-form estimations. Structural estimations proceeded with and without inclusion of reaction functions describing the policymakers' endogenous responses. It would appear that structural estimates are comparatively little affected by nonrecognition of endogenous policy responses. Direct estimation of the system's (exclusive of reaction functions) reduced form produces, in contrast, seriously biased multiplier estimates.

We should hardly quibble with the correctness of the argument advanced by Goldfeld and Blinder. Endogenous policy responses *can* yield seriously biased estimates of reduced forms exemplified by Eq. (1). The meaning of this result must be carefully assessed, however. The authors usefully sharpen our awareness for some important qualifications applicable to the empirical work which emerged in the context of the "fiscalist debate." The results hold for classes of hypotheses recognizing an actual state of comparative exogeneity with respect to policy variables. Goldfeld and Blinder offer no argument or evidence bearing on the crucial issues of *whether, when* and *how* "policy was endogenous." The correctness of their analysis does not, unfortunately, establish its relevance. We still need to judge the occurrence and nature of endogenous policy responses. It is important to understand, however, that judgments based purely on standard regression analyses can seriously mislead us. We also need to examine carefully the institutional arrangements and explore special events in the manner of Friedman and Schwartz (1963). Institutional information may often tell us what regressions, if any, are advisable. A "mechanical" linking of policy variables with a GNP gap hardly conforms to institutional situations prevailing over most periods or in most countries. The data used in regression estimates of Eq. (1) by various researchers covered a variety of historical episodes and also different countries. One would conjecture that the existing institutional differences generate widely different endogenous responses. A consistent pattern of statistical results over periods and countries deserve more serious considerations under the circumstances, even with full acknowledgment of the argument advanced by Goldfeld and Blinder. It is very doubtful for instance that past episodes of U.S. fiscal and monetary history exhibit a pronounced and approximately uniform stabilization policy. The available information about the Fed's strategy and tactical procedure suggests, moreover, the operation of a major random process affecting monetary growth over quarterly periods. This situation may, for all practical purposes, amount to an approximate exogeneity actually emphasized by Goldfeld and Blinder. The political economy of fiscal policy also suggests substantial doubts about the relevant occurrence of an endogenous fixed stabilization policy. "Stabilization" may be a useful rhetoric device addressed to academics and the public arena. But fiscal policy is dominated by other considerations associated with the incentive structure characterizing the existing policy institutions. This incentive structure implies that "fiscal policy" is dominated by redistributional interests with little substantive attention to "stabilization" per se. We should expect under the circumstances that regressions expressing fiscal reaction functions remain poorly defined and unstable over time. We may, of course, encounter situations justifying a substantial suspicion that endogenous policy responses do occur. But the implications with respect to estimates of Eq. (1) are obscure until we know more about the nature of endogenous policy patterns. Information about occurrence only establishes that we need be cautious in interpreting the results. But Goldfeld and Blinder still enriched our discussion. This contribution warms us essentially to extend the empirical work to as many different periods and situations involving different institutional arrangements as possible. This research strategy seems more promising than an approach relying on explicit statistical reaction functions of the usual kind embedded in a large structural model.

2.1.e. Some problems of statistical theory. A retrospective evaluation guided by an interest to learn from the previous discussions for our present purposes cannot avoid an application of standards—criteria of procedures developed subsequent to the discussion under examination. Two aspects bearing on statistical procedures and matters of statistical theory require our attention. Most of the discussants used level data; Ando and Modigliani and De Prano and Mayer used data only in this form. Friedman and Meiselman also explored first differences, whereas Andersen and Jordan only used first differences. The proper choice between these alternative procedures poses a subtle but very important and widely neglected issue even today. The choice depends sensitively on the error structure in the formulated regression (Plosser and Schwert 1978) or the nonstationarity of the variables (Meese and Singleton 1982). Plosser and Schwert compared the problems posed by over- and under-differencing of data in regression analysis. They explore, in particular, the asymmetric effect of over- and under-differencing on statistical inferences. They show that over-differencing produces a regression with an error term controlled by an $MA(1)$ process with a unit coefficient, whereas under-differencing yields a regression with a nonstationary random term. Over-differencing still allows, under the circumstances, reliable estimation and inferences. Under-differencing, in contrast, poses a serious problem. The sample distribution of the estimator does not possess finite moments. No inferences are possible in this case.

The authors elaborate the general problem with the aid of several examples bearing quite directly on our issue. The first example explores a regression $\log y = \alpha + \beta \log m + \epsilon$, with y representing nominal income and m the money stock. The regression is estimated in level form, in levels modified with a time trend, with Cochrane–Orcutt adjustment, and also in first and second differences. The last four procedures yield essentially the same estimate for β. The first estimate derived from level data is separated by more than two standard errors from the estimate obtained on the basis of first differences. Most interesting is a comparison of the variances computed for the error term in the regressions. Over-differencing would imply that the variance associated with the first difference is twice the variance of the residual in the level regression. Under-differencing implies, in contrast, that the residual variance in the level regression exceeds the corresponding variance in the first difference. This implication is confirmed by the estimates.

The authors contrast this case with the "quantity theory of sunspots" expressed by the regression $\log y = \alpha + \beta \log s + \epsilon$, where s measures the accumulated sum of sunspots. The same five estimation procedures, previously mentioned were carried out. The results based on level data convey the impression of a significant relation with a substantial correlation and a unit multiplier. The first difference yields a radically different result. The "multiplier" β-coefficient collapses to nonsignificance with a standard error almost equal to the coefficient estimate. The estimate derived from the second difference collapses even further and is hardly distinguishable from zero. The residual variance in the level regression is, moreover, almost 13 times the residual variance in first differences.

Lastly, the authors examine the data (A and M—in logs, however) used by Friedman and Meiselman. They compare the regressions $\log C = \alpha + \beta \log M + \epsilon$ with $\log C = \gamma + \delta \log A + \partial$. The results are remarkably different. The five estimation procedures yield the same results for β. The differences are not statistically significant when evaluated in terms of the standard error of β computed from first differences. Once again the residual variance of the level regression sub-stantially exceeds this variance of the first differences. This pattern of residual variances occurs even more emphatically in the case of auto-nomous expenditures. The contrast offered by this regression appears, however, most particularly in the pattern of δ-estimates associated with the five estimation procedures. The coefficient collapses from 1.08 in level data to 0.14 in first differences and 0.09 in second differences. The differences in estimates are statistically highly significant. *All* estimates remain, however, significantly different from zero.

This analysis with the examples immediately related to our problem clearly reveals the danger associated with under-differencing and the misleading inferences obtainable under these circumstances. The results developed by Plosser and Schwert suggest a definite strategy for empirical investigations, at least in our range of problems. In the usual absence of sufficient information about the error structure we need to estimate both in terms of level data (unadjusted and adjusted for possible serial correla-tion in residuals), first differences, and, possibly, even second differences. The resulting pattern of residual variances and coefficient estimates deter-mines our evaluation. A residual variance of level regressions substantially higher than the corresponding variance associated with first differences suggests the relevant application of first differences. The regression obtained from level data should, moreover, be considered seriously suspect whenever the estimated regression coefficients substantially collapse for first and second differences. It follows thus that the results presented by Ando and Modigliani or De Prano and Mayer yield little information until further reevaluation.

A possibly more basic problem was raised by Meese and Singleton (1982) and Wasserfallen (1985). The standard assumptions for regression analysis are satisfied for stationary stochastic variables and nonstochastic independent variables. The latter case hardly applies to a relevant analysis of data cast up by social processes. But nonstationary stochastic data pose a serious problem for estimation and inferences. It would appear that consistent estimates of a regression require that the diagonal terms of the covariance matrix of independent *exogenous* variables converge to infinity with the sample size. Alternatively, it seems sufficient that the independent (and exogenous) vector variable be controlled by a *finite* autoregressive process. These conditions offer, however, no basis for inferences. More structure must be imposed in order to derive an asymptotic sampling distribution. The weakest condition on the moment matrix of independent variables seems to have been formulated, according to Meese and Singleton, by Grenander (1954): "These conditions preclude exponential growth of any variable.... Borderline non-stationarity (i.e., unit root) is allowed if regressors are fixed or strictly exogenous." Meese and Singleton emphasize that an independent error with finite variance is not a sufficient condition for asymptotic inferences. Quite generally, conditions on the regressors required for deriving inferences pose a troublesome issue. In the absence of good grounds supporting the relevant application of asymptotic distribution theory to inferences derived from nonstationary data, we may possibly obtain estimates but no judgment on evaluation. This argument reenforces the conclusion obtained from Plosser and Schwert's investigation: It seems advisable in the case of nonstationary data to derive the inferences from suitable transformation into stationary series. The neglect of this problem lowers the relevance of some empirical work presented in the "fiscalist" debate.

2.1.f. Some general conditions. We should emphasize first that Johnson's indictment, recently repeated by Tobin after more than ten years, simply has no foundation. It reflects a somewhat casual misunderstanding of the nature of the argument. Friedman and Meiselman explicitly cautioned the reader that this assessment was quite provisional. It was also a definitely limited examination, and so was the work undertaken at the Federal Reserve Bank of St. Louis. The limitation is defined by the class of hypotheses implicitly addressed by the tests used. There do exist classes of hypotheses that cannot be subsumed under the assessments carried out. Friedman and Meiselman properly stressed therefore that their results are "not decisive." They are certainly not decisive with respect to the general paradigm and the general idea of fiscal effects on aggregate demand. But the tests were properly formulated and executed *relative* to the class of hypotheses considered. A reservation should be entered, however, with respect to the use of under-differenced and nonstationary variables. We should also note the reservation advanced by Goldfeld and Blinder. This reservation simply suggests some further examination in order to take account of potential effects of endogenous policy reactions.

The discussion also brought forth a perennial problem confronting our empirical work. The choice of exogenous variables forms an important component in the construction of a hypothesis (or class of hypotheses). The development of statistical analysis has sharpened somewhat our understanding and offered approaches to this issue. One lesson we should emphatically learn in this context emphasizes that we need to address more careful attention to the admissible interpretation of our work. Our imaginative invention of alternative specifications or constructions of exogenous magnitudes offers per se no rational grounds for the rejection of other specifications and choices. We need either (more or less) direct evidence bearing on the exogeneity of the variables concerned or to depend on the evaluation of the hypothesis as a whole. Correlation statements may appear as relevant test statements in this context, provided, however, as in the case of the core class examined by Friedman and Meiselman, the hypothesis under consideration *implies* comparative correlation statements. Comparison of correlations in the absence of such definite implications is meaningless and without any evidential value.

The substantive content of the discussion contributed in retrospect to some clarification. The hard Keynesian position dismissing monetary conditions was unanimously discarded. The relevance of monetary conditions became generally recognized. Substantial issues remained, however, in this range. Some Keynesians argued that the money stock or monetary growth exerts "permanent" (long-lasting) real effects. Monetarists confine, in contrast, (temporary) real effects to monetary acceleration (or decelerations). More important for our immediate purpose was the general recognition that fiscal policy did probably modify to some extent nominal aggregate demand for output. Substantial differences concerning orders of magnitude and persistence of real effects remained.

There occurred also a subtle but interesting shift within the Keynesian paradigm. This shift modified the meaning of "fiscal dominance." We observe well into the 1950s an argument assigning a steep slope to the IS curve and a flat slope to the LM curve. This assignment was justified in terms of a borrowing-cost interpretation for the interest elasticity of aggregate demand (Brunner 1971). There clearly emerged a revision of this position during the 1960s. The relative slopes shifted sufficiently to offer monetary conditions a significant leverage. The inherited sense of "fiscal dominance" unavoidably disappeared. The appearance of the assignment problem and the policy mix analysis reveals this change. But the modified Keynesian analysis produced a new sense of "fiscal dominance" visible in the "Economic Reports" of the Kennedy–Johnson administration. Both monetary and fiscal policies were recognized to influence real magnitudes. Both policies were thus in principle applicable to stabilization purposes. Monetary policy was, however, judged to concentrate the social cost of stabilization policies on a small segment of the economy (housing). Fiscal policy, in contrast, spread these costs more "equitably." Fiscal policy was also judged to operate "directly," in contrast to the "indirect" effects of monetary policy, and, consequently, with shorter lags. These considerations determined that fiscal policy was proposed as the active component of a stabilization program with monetary policy assigned an essentially accommodating role defined in terms of an interest-rate strategy. This position was sensitively conditioned by the underlying paradigm summarized by the IS/LM approach and its economic interpretation. This paradigm with its confining view about the nature of the "transmission mechanism" remained, of course, on center stage in the dispute between "Keynesians" and "monetarists."

2.2. *The asset market effects of fiscal policy and the stability of the system*

The discussion covered in the previous paragraphs addressed the comparatively immediate output-market effects of fiscal policy. Neither Keynesians nor monetarists had at this stage integrated the ramifications of deficit financing via asset-market responses explicitly into their analysis. Attention focused by the early 1970s on the government's budget constraint. The relation between fiscal policy and asset-market responses generated by the mode of deficit financing and the resulting interaction between asset markets and output markets became the subject of further examination (Christ 1979; Silber 1970; Blinder and Solow 1974, 1976; Infante and Stein 1976; Brunner and Meltzer 1972b, 1976; McCallum 1981). The participants in this discussion agreed that fiscal policy (including especially the effects of distortionary taxes and the *structure* of expenditures) affects actual output, normal output, price level, and real rates of interest. There remained, however, substantial variations in the details of the analysis and probably the order of magnitudes involved. The question pursued was addressed to the real and nominal consequences implicit in fiscal decisions beyond the effects attributable to (global) expenditures and taxes per se.

My summary of the issue exploits a scheme used in various papers by Brunner and Meltzer. The scheme involves an interaction between four lines represented in Figure 3.1. The vertical line describes normal output. Some strands of analysis recognized the dependence of the line's position on taxes and most particularly on longer-run portfolio adjustments between government securities and real capital. The *bbe* line represents the balanced budget equation. It describes thus the locus of price level and output combinations (p,y) that satisfy a balanced budget. The position of the line depends on real government expenditures, the stock of outstanding debt held by the public, and a tax parameter. The slope of the line expresses the nonhomogeneity of the deficit function due to progressive taxation, yielding a "bracket creep." Under proportional taxation the *bbe* line would be vertical. The *d*-line presents a pseudodemand curve to be understood in a semireduced sense. The line summarizes the locus of all pairs (p,y) that satisfy simultaneously, for any given set of other variables, output- and asset-market equations. Lastly, the *s*-line describes the "structural" supply function. The position of this line moves with the expected price level, the stock of real capital, and technological progress.

The initial position in the diagram shows a state of full stock and normal output equilibrium. The short-run flow equilibrium determined by the interaction between pseudodemand and supply yields a state on the normal output line that simultaneously produces a balanced budget. Now

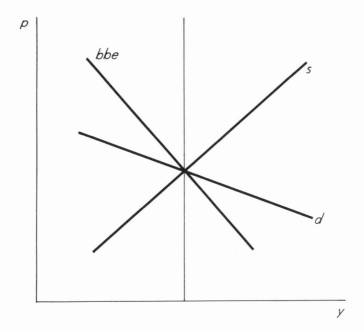

Figure 3.1

consider an increase in real government expenditures (or a lower tax parameter). This raises the balanced budget line to the position bbe_1, and the pseudodemand line to d_1 (see Figure 3.2). The fiscal stimulus thus immediately raises output, price level, and interest rates. It also produces a deficit expressed by the distance of the *bbe* line from point *A*, which describes the new flow equilibrium. Suppose for the moment that the deficit is financed with a new issue of government bonds. The resulting increase in the stock of securities and interest rates pushes the *bbe* line further upward along the (vertical) normal output line. The net effect of a bond-financed deficit thus depends crucially on the interaction between asset markets and output markets. This interaction determines the movement of the pseudodemand curve relative to the balanced budget line induced by the fiscal action. The result depends, within the context of the IS/LM framework, on the relative magnitude of the vertical shifts imposed on the two curves. A comparatively larger upward shift of the IS curve due to wealth effects induced by the bond issue raises the *d*-line, whereas a comparatively larger wealth effect operating on the LM curve lowers the line. The Brunner–Meltzer asset-market analysis yields a somewhat more complex pattern modifying the wealth effect with substitution effects between financial and real assets. The absorption of a larger stock of government securities by the asset markets unleashes offsetting

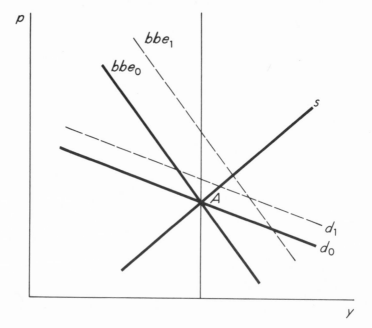

Figure 3.2

influences via interest rates on financial assets and via the asset price of real assets. The net effect thus remains quite ambiguous without constraining order conditions. Neither argument thus yields, without specific order constraints, a definite answer. Even a positive response of the d-line is not sufficient, however, for the stability of the stock equilibrium. This stability requires that the upward shift in the d-line caused by deficit finance exceed the corresponding upward shift of the bbe-line. This conditions assures that the d-line eventually catches up with the bbe-line, and the flow equilibrium produces a balanced budget.

Some variations in the analysis occur at this point. Some authors emphasize the transitory nature of movements along the s-curve. The latter will shift upward in response to adjustments in the expected price level. The final state of equilibrium will thus tend to the normal output line. But the conditions for stability appear under either the IS/LM or the Brunner–Meltzer analysis quite unlikely. Instability associated with insufficient nonnegative or even negative responses of the d-line appear more likely in the context of both analytic arguments.

In contrast, consider the case of a deficit financed with new base money. The d-line is definitely raised, whereas the bbe-line is not further raised by the increase in the money stock associated with deficit finance. The stability of the stock equilibrium is thus ensured under the circumstances. The d-line eventually intersects the bbe-line on the vertical. Several aspects should be noted here. The total effect on the price level (and on output in case the nature-rate hypothesis is rejected) is a multiple of the "immediate" effect associated with the flow equilibrium response to a fiscal impulse. The latter is described by the shift of the state point to point A, whereas the final state of stock equilibrium is controlled by the intersection of the budget line and the normal output line. The total effect of a bond-financed deficit is even large in case the stability conditions is imposed. This follows from the fact that the bbe-line moves during the adjust process beyond the position determined by the initial rise in real government expenditures. The total effect thus reflects in both cases the *financial* repercussions of fiscal policy decisions.

The implications of the more likely *unstable* bond-financed deficit process deserve some more attention. Carl Christ (1979) emphasized that this result poses a problem for the imposition of a monetary rule. Such a rule confines the proportion of the deficit financed with base money below the critical level, assuring stability of the stock adjustment process whenever the deficit is sufficiently large. Brunner (1976) and, recently, McCallum (1981) emphasized the (partial) alleviation of the problem produced by economic growth. Such growth moves the flow equilibrium with the normal output line to the right and closes the gap between the state point fixed by the flow equilibrium and a given budget line. For any given normal growth rate there exists an upper limit on the growth of real debt (and thus of the deficit) beyond which economic growth cannot produce stability; that is, the movement of the *bbe*-line to the right exceeds the growth-determined shift to the flow equilibrium. We should also consider that the analysis implies a negative effect of bond-financed deficits on the rate of normal growth via the longer-run adjustments in the stock of real capital.

But deficits beyond the critical level appear substantially more likely today than ten years ago. A low-level monetary growth would thus induce with substantial probability the unstable process discussed above. This process would raise real and nominal interest rates over time and lower the normal rate of real growth. None of these consequences induces within the economic system, according to either type of analysis, any feedbacks eventually terminating the process. However, we need to broaden our vision at this state and admit the interaction with the political process. The persistent increase in the real debt raises real interest rates and the relative burden of interest payments expressed by the ratio of interest payments to national income. This trend eventually induces rejection of low-level monetary growth in order to moderate the growth in real debt or even lower this stock with the aid of a higher price level. A change in fiscal regime offers an alternative avenue. The crucial conclusion from this stability analysis suggests that a stable noninflationary monetary regime is unlikely to persist in the absence of a *fiscal* regime effectively containing the average deficit. Both monetarist and Keynesian analysis developed at the time implied that the fiscal regime determines the longer-run opportunities of monetary policy. Alternatively, proposals for a *monetary* rule require supplementary proposal for a *fiscal* rule.

3. The "NeoClassical" Contribution

The last phases of the discussion summarized in the previous section overlapped with a new thrust in fiscal policy analysis. The "rational expectations revolution" also influenced, beyond the approach to monetary analysis, the analysis of the government's fiscal policy. A series of articles by Robert Barro, beginning in 1978, introduced a "neoclassical vision" into our discussion. The emerging analysis radically changed the economic significance of deficits. Deficits were interpreted similar to the deviations between *current* income and *current* consumption of private households in the context of an intertemporal allocation. The public debt and its behavior thus reflects the public sector's intertemporal optimization conditioned by the pattern of permanent and transitory government expenditures. But decisions to issue bonds in order to finance expenditures affect, in contrast to both Keynesian and monetarist analyses, neither real interest reates nor the price level nor, even temporarily, output and employment. The stability issue discussed above does not exist under the circumstances. Traditional notions of stabilization thus offer no relevant motivation for public debt policy. This position bearing on deficits and debt does not extend to government expenditures on goods and services and "non-lump-sum" taxation. Budgetary policies expressed by expenditure and tax decisions do exert temporary and permanent real effects. This analysis, most especially developed by Barro (1981a), actually involved aspects of government budgetary operations, which, even if known in a general sense, were long neglected by macroanalysis. Standard macrotheory typically presented the public sector as a sinkhole for goods and services produced by the private sector. Martin Bailey moved beyond this "sinkhole theory" of the government sector and considered the government's supply of goods and services to the private sector. The substitutive or complementary nature of this supply with respect to private consumption and investment may substantially modify the traditional results. Barro (1981b, 1984a) revived Bailey's neglected initiative and also elaborated more carefully the impact of non-lump-sum taxation. He also revived in this context some earlier work by Miller and Upton (1974). The analysis addressed, beyond these aspects, different mechanisms yielding the real effects of budgetary decisions. It shares with monetary analysis an emphasis on wealth and substitution effects, in contrast to the Keynesian reliance on the income multiplier. Its emphasis on perpetual market clearing relative to *all* ongoing shocks differentiates it from both Keynesian and monetarist arguments.

3.1. The "Ricardian Theme"

Barro must be credited for having revived a theme originally considered by Ricardo. The stability analysis examined above assumed that the financial decision between bonds and taxes exert a permanent real effect. Barro's argument persuasively challenges this position. He emphasizes that the traditional argument neglects to incorporate the future tax liability associated with current borrowing. A careful separation of issues requires, in this context, the assumption of lump-sum taxes. This assumption permits us to isolate the possible effects attributable to financial decision as such without contamination with the real effects of distortionary taxes. The forward-looking behavior emphasized by rational expectations interprets deficit finance essentially as an intertemporal reallocation of taxes. This implies that current deficits, expressed by a new sale of bonds, correspond to a shift of taxes from the present to the future. The present value of the forfeited (current) tax thus equals the present value of the future tax liability. This equality holds under an important assumption introduced by Barro and discussed subsequently. It holds, in particular, whether the bonds issues are maturing at a specified recognized date, according to a contingent state pattern (Chan 1983), according to a probability pattern over time, or, lastly, whether the bonds are perpetuities.

The "Ricardian argument" requires the formal apparatus of intertemporal budget constraints for both a representative household and government. A first simple argument confines the repayment period of debt to the representative taxpayers economic horizon. This constraint can be used to demonstrate that the present value of the future (expected) government expenditures plus the inherited government debt are equal to the present value of expected future taxes. Similarly, the household's budget constraint shows that the sum of present value of expected future consumption and the present value of expected future taxes is equal to the present value of expected future income plus inherited assets. Any temporal reallocation of taxes combined with an unchanged stream of government expenditures produces an equality between current non-tax-financed government expenditures and the present value of future changes in tax liabilities. This result follows from the government's budget constraint. It implies in conjunction with the budget constraint of the representative household that the household's real opportunities are invariant with respect to the deficit. The household's wealth position defined by its present value of consumption remains unaffected and so does the present value of taxes and income. Households find the optimal choice of consumption pattern unchanged under the circumstances. The creation of a deficit thus cannot modify household consumption decisions. Substitution effects induced by distorting incentives are, moreover, excluded by the lump-sum character of taxes. The household's prior optimal consumption plan extends to the new situation, whatever the representative household's utility function may be. The deficit thus induces neither an intertemporal substitution nor a scale effect on consumption. The current deficit is perfectly matched under the circumstances by an increase in household saving. The government sector's dissaving is thus fully offset by additional private saving. The economy's total saving is therefore independent of the government's financial decision. This saving provides the necessary funds to absorb the new bonds into the household's portfolio. Optimal portfolio management determines this link between deficits, household saving, and bond acquisitions as a consequence of rational hedging. With portfolios optimally adjusted in terms of risk–return combinations before the new deficit emerges, households will find it advisable to hedge the expected tax liability by acquiring a corresponding amount of bonds. The optimal portfolio position will thus be maintained. In terms of the Brunner–Meltzer asset-market model, this result implies that the public's net (stock) supply of government securities disappears in the credit-market equation. It follows that variations in the stock of government securities exert no effects on asset markets. Asset prices and interest rates will not be affected. It follows, moreover, with respect to the stability analysis of Section 2 that the *d*-line remains unaffected by the government's debt finance.

The argument establishing the Ricardian thesis is crucially conditioned by the two budget constraints. These constraints involve several important assumptions that decisively determine the conclusions. Barro explored these assumptions in careful detail and argued persuasively their a priori reasonableness as a good approximation to reality. Buiter and Tobin (1978) and Tobin (1980) examined the underlying assumption with a matching vigor and argued persuasively their a priori unreasonableness as an approach to reality. There is no need to reproduce these excellent discussions here in depth. My comments concentrate on three aspects associated with the intertemporal budget constraints. These aspects bear on the horizon of the representative household, the nature of capital markets, and risks or uncertainties associated with deficit finance.

The simple fact of mortality combined with our knowledge of demographic structure and debt policies destroys the assumption that the representative household's horizon is at least as long as the repayment period of debt associated with a given tax cut. An "infinitely" living household would circumvent this problem for the Ricardian theme. Barro provided a subtle and extensive analysis interpreting this assumption in empirical terms. He introduced the notion of "operative intergenerational bequests and transfers" to link finitely living generations within an infinitely operating household. This is achieved analytically with an ingenious device. The utility of each generation depends on the utility level of the next generation. The implicit nesting of utility functions yields the appearance of an infinitely living decision unit. This does not imply that the consumption of future generations is equally weighted as the present generation's own consumption. Its implication denies, however, the dependence of consumption pattern on age characteristics of life cycle theories. Optimal consumption choices of infinitely living households produce a preferred pattern of intergenerational transfers (in either direction). Any intrusion by the government to modify this pattern via its budgetary operations necessarily fails under the circumstances. Impositions of tax burdens on future generations via a bond-financed deficit induces offsetting transfer of wealth from the present to the future generation financed with the additional current saving produced by the tax cut. The voluntarily determined optimal pattern of intergenerational transfers dominates the outcome and overrides or offsets the government's budgetary operations. The extension to an infinite budget constraint still assures that any cut in current taxes is exactly balanced by the present value of future tax liabilities. A shifting of the tax incidence beyond a mortal man's life span does not change his optimal intertemporal choice. The initial choice prevailing before the intertemporal tax shift remains optimal. This result implies that current tax cuts yield no wealth effects on current consumption or other real variables.

3.2. The Ricardian Theme: Its qualification

3.2.a. Intergenerational altruism and intergenerational selfishness. The invariance of intergenerational transfers with respect to budgetary operations is crucially conditioned by the assumption of "intergenerational altruism." This assumption justifies the infinite horizon. Consider, in contrast, the opposite assumption, "intergenerational selfishness," combined with the life cycle hypothesis of consumption (Kotlikoff 1984). The latter hypothesis implies that the marginal propensity to consume increases with age. The assumption of "intergenerational selfishness" reenforces this pattern as older generations plan no bequests under the circumstances. Any transfer between generations modifies in this case aggregate real consumption. In particular, a transfer from the younger to the older generation raises aggregate consumption. A shift in taxes from the old to the young would produce this result. Replacing some current taxes with bonds maturing during the young generation's lifetime after the older generation's death would accomplish the necessary shift. The result emerges with even larger weight whenever the future tax liabilities fall on unborn generations. "Intergenerational selfishness" thus assures that any temporal reallocation associated with a deficit induces intergenerational transfer not "washed out" within an infinite intertemporal budget constraint. The intergenerational transfers are not offset and produce real consequences. They actually modify the relevant budget constraint for each generation.

The difference between the two cases may be conveyed in the following terms. Let the expression

$$A_{i+1} + C_i + T_i = Y_i + A_i$$

denote the *i*th generation's budget constraint, where A_{i+1} indicates the bequests transmitted to generation $i+1$ by generation *i*. C_i, T_i, and Y_i describe the present value (as of generation 0) of consumption, taxes, and income for generations *i* over its lifetime. With intergenerational altruism A_1 reflects the optimal transfer decisions in response to changes in T_0 and the matching changes in T_1. Thus follows the relevance of the infinite budget constraint. Intergenerational selfishness breaks up this pattern. Its strict and narrow application means that $A_{i+1} = 0$. A change in T_0 thus invariably induces a change in C_0 that exceeds, with the differential in marginal propensities, the change in C_1 in the initial period.

This analysis suffers, however, in comparison with the "intergenerational altruism" model from some immediate confrontation with reality. We do observe that wealth is actually transmitted from one generation to another. These transfers are excluded by the narrowly formulated "selfishness model." The occurrence of transfers is, however, not necessarily an expression of *voluntary* and *planned* transfers associated with intergenerational altruism once we move beyond the context of perfect information. Blanchard (1984) argued that an insurance scheme under risk yields the same result of no bequests. But such insurance does either not exist (specifically the one used by Blanchard) or it at most only used or offered partially by agents. But bequests apparently do occur. The context of risk could explain, however, the *appearance* of bequest without the bequest *motive* as formalized by Barro. Agents face some probability that the remaining life span exceeds the expected time. Risk averse agents will therefore adjust the use of their wealth in view of this uncertainty. Their problem is similar to the asymmetric risks associated occasionally with inventory decision. The asymmetry is probably even more acute in this case. Using up all resources before death exposes a person to serious hazards. This is balanced by unused resources at death, reflecting lowered consumption before death. The comparatively lower level of consumption can be understood as a premium paid for self-insurance against the hazards of early exhaustion of one's resources. Wealth will be held under the circumstances beyond the requirements of the statistical expectations bearing on the remaining life span. It follows that, on average, unused wealth will be transmitted at death to the next generation without an "operative bequest motive." Intergenerational transfers operated by budget deficits would in this case still raise current consumption. The observation of substantial intergenerational transmission of wealth is thus consistent with the denial of "Ricardian equivalence."

It should be noted that this argument disregards the potential role of annuities to be purchased by the older generation. But even an actuarially fair supply of annuities would probably not completely replace the holding of tradeable wealth as insurance for old age hazards expressed by only partially insurable large expenses on health problems. The annuity business, moreover, operates at a cost. A comparison of this cost with the cost of self-insurance could be expected to have a margin of tradeable wealth. But an entirely different argument, developed by Bernheim, Shleifer, and Summers (1985), explicitly recognizes the occurrence of voluntary planned bequests and offers probably a more relevant critique of the Ricardian thesis of debt neutrality. This analysis will be examined in subsequent sections covering the empirical work.

3.2.b. Corner solutions. The alternative hypotheses yield very different interpretations of social security. The Ricardian theme implies that such arrangements are offset by correspondingly larger transfers from the older to the next generation with no effect on current consumption. The alternative, articulated by Feldstein (1982), implies that this intergenerational transfer raises current consumption. An interesting explanation of the emergence of social security (Meltzer and Richard 1985) reenforces the "non-Ricardian" hypothesis. Social security is interpreted as a substitute for the voluntary social arrangements made within the larger family. Social evolution gradually eroded such arrangements and raised the older generation's control problem associated with the extraction of the support. Social security emerged as a political solution to this problem. This explanation cannot be reconciled with a Ricardian equivalence. Its basic structure asserts, on the contrary, that the intergenerational link described by Barro has been suspended. This interpretation suggests, moreover, the occurrence of several important facts bearing on intergenerational transfers. Such transfers do not occur solely in the form of a tradeable wealth accumulated by the older generation and eventually inherited by the younger generation. Voluntary intergenerational transfers may frequently involve an intertemporal exchange between older and younger generations. The older generation invests initially in health, education, and other dimensions of the younger generation with the expectation of support (i.e., negative bequests) during old age. The extraction of support does not proceed without control and transactions costs, however. The hypothesis indicated above states basically that specifiable social changes raised these costs and increased the likelihood of corner solutions when unrestricted optimality yields negative bequests. Under the circumstances the government's intervention increases current real consumption. Lastly, we note that this argument also suggests that a single representative household does not adequately represent the actual diversity encountered in matters of intergenerational transfers.

The representative household's infinite intertemporal budget constraint requires, in addition to the special intergenerational link, an assumption about capital markets. This assumption removes the occurrence of another solution. The representative household's lending and borrowing rates coincide with the rates available to the government's operation. A violation of this conditions produces wealth effects that suspend the Ricardian equivalence. Chan (1983) explored this theme in the context of an assumption approximating the problem in terms of liquidity constraints imposed on a subset of households. A debt-financed deficit operates under the circumstances to substitute government borrowing for constrained household borrowing. Households with no liquidity constraint or a nonbinding one respond to the deficit and its finance in the "Ricardian manner" with the offsetting behavior discussed above. Households suffering binding liquidity constraints before the event experience, through the intermediation of the government, a relaxation of the constraint. They will react by shifting future consumption into current consumption. The distribution of significant liquidity constraints or the distribution of differential borrowing rates of interest between government and households determines the net effect of a debt-financed tax cut on households' current consumption.

Some fundamental theoretical exploration about the conditions for Barro's "operative intergenerational bequests" qualifies the debt neutrality result. Barro's analysis is conditioned by the assumption that intergenerational transfers from old to young occur independently of debt. The emergence of debt changes neither opportunities nor preferences in the world described. No real consequences thus ensue. An interior solution is simply maintained. Philippe Weil (1984) examined the problem with great analytic care. His basic theme emphasizes the existence of a "deep connection between the efficiency properties of overlapping generation economies without bequest motive and the possible direction of intergenerational transfers." There exist, in particular, overlapping generation economies that "justify," in terms of efficiency, intergenerational transfers from young to old. Weil demonstrates that the existence of "operative bequests" in a suitably defined steady state depends on the discount applies by the old to the future utility of the young. This discount should not exceed a benchmark determined by the gap between the interest rate and economic growth in a diamond-type model. Weil concludes that a "wide class of economies with a bequest motive" do not satisfy Barro's proposition about Ricardian debt neutrality. The limited significance of this analysis should be clearly understood. It essentially establishes that Barro's result is nonvacuous and places necessary and sufficient conditions on its occurrence. This purely analytic result cannot settle the crucial empirical issue at stake.

3.2.c. Risk and uncertainty. Risk and uncertainty are essentially exorcised from the argument supporting the Ricardian theme. A firm link connects the household's benefits from the current tax cut with the future tax burden. The government's infinite intertemporal budget constraint also removes all risk and uncertainty with regard to the government's budgetary operation. Agents can rest assured that future tax liabilities guarantee the crucial equality of present values.

The pattern is substantially modified once we admit risk and uncertainty on two levels into the analysis. Barro (1981a) and Feldstein (1982) already noted in passing some consequences associated with uncertainty about the households' future tax liability. Barro suggested that uncertainty raises the perception of the present value attached to future tax liabilities by risk-averse households. Thus a debt-financed deficit *lowers* under uncertain future tax liabilities the representative household's perception of its wealth position. Current private consumption thus *declines* as a result of the deficit. The suggestive remark was developed by Chan (1983) in some explicit analytic detail. The argument still adheres to a state of lump-sum taxes with certainty concerning the future *aggregate* tax liability. Households suffer, however, incomplete information and consequently experience some risk about the distribution of the global burden among the taxpayers. The *individual* household's future tax burden is determined by a stochastic process. It follows that the individual's share of the current tax cut does not match his share of the future tax liability. This suspension of the crucial link produced by a stochastic tax incidence implies, under conventional restrictions on preferences, that a debt-financed deficit *lowers* current consumption. The larger the uncertainty about the incidence of the future tax liabilities, moreover, the *larger* is the negative effect of a deficit on current consumption. The result reveals that households hedge against the risk imposed on them by saving even more than determined under certainty. The hedging response induces a substitution of saving at the *expense* of consumption.

A similar theme, but different in its conclusion, was recently developed by Barsky, Mankiw, and Zeldes (1984). Risk-averse households encounter in this case not an uncertain tax incidence but an uncertain future income. An intertemporal reallocation of tax liabilities (with less now and more in the future) lowers the degree of uncertainty bearing on future income. The precautionary demand for savings declines and real consumption *increases* under the circumstances. This result is, moreover, produced under strict "Ricardian conditions."

The analysis proceeds in the context of a two-period model characterized by three budget constraints. The two constraints describing the household's position appear as

$$W_1 = \mu_1 - C_1, \tag{2}$$

$$C_2 = (1 + R) W_1 + \mu_2 + \epsilon_2, \tag{3}$$

where C_1 and C_2 refer to consumption in periods 1 and 2, μ_1 and $\mu_2 + \epsilon_2$ designate income in the two periods, W_1 defines savings in period 1, and R is the interest rate. The magnitudes μ_1 and μ_2 are nonstochastic, whereas ϵ is the stochastic component of future income. A temporal tax shift is introduced by inserting T *positively* in Eq. (2) and $(1 + R)T$ *nega-*

tively in Eq. (3) The signs are determined by the fact that any initial tax burden is impounded into μ_2 and μ_2. We thus rewrite the household's budget constraints as

$$W_1 = \mu_1 + T - C_1, \tag{4}$$

$$C_2 = (1 + R)W_1 - (1 + R)T + \mu_2 + \epsilon. \tag{5}$$

The government needs to levy taxes in the second period in order to finance the repayment of $(1 + R)T$. The required tax rate is thus determined by the relation

$$(1 + R)T = t\mu_2. \tag{6}$$

The revenues from extra taxation imposed on expected income should cover the repayment. The actual tax revenue is

$$t(\mu_2 + \epsilon_2) = (1 + R)T + \frac{(1 + R)T}{\mu_2}\epsilon_2.$$

The second period's household constraint can thus be rewritten once more as

$$C_2 = (1 + R)W - (1 + R)T + \mu_2 + [1 - \frac{(1 + R)T}{\mu_2}]\epsilon. \tag{7}$$

Lastly, the authors postulate a three-times differentiable utility function in C_1 and C_2 satisfying the conditions

$$(1 + R)U_{222} - U_{122} > 0.$$

The first-order optimality conditions are immediately derived:

$$EU_1(C_1, C_2) = (1 + R)EU_2(C_1, C_2).$$

A straightforward manipulation of this condition yields the marginal propensity to consume:

$$\frac{\partial C_1}{\partial T} = \frac{(1 + R)Cov[(1 + R)U_{22} - U_{12}, \epsilon]}{-\mu_2[EU_{11} - \partial(1 + R)EU_{12} + (1 + R)^2 EU_{22}]} > 0. \tag{8}$$

A reduction in current taxes, appearing as a position magnitude in the constraint, thus *raises* current consumption. Tax policies induce, under the circumstances, specified real effects in the economy. These effects emerge even with the households' definite perception that the present value of its expected future tax liabilities equals the taxes foregone in the present. The result is crucially conditioned by the positive covariance term in Eq. (8). This result vanishes in the absence of the third-order derivative condition imposed on the utility function. Once we accept this condition the crucial aspect centers on the reduction in the variance of second-period income produced by a nonvanishing tax rate $t = (1 + R)T/\mu_2$. The variance is actually reduced in the proportion $(1 - t)^2$.

The authors offer two distinct interpretations for the two-period model. One confines the model to the lifetime of a single individual. Income uncertainty bears in this case on an individual's uncertainty within the life cycle. The other interpretations introduce intergenerational relations. The second period refers to the economic uncertainty attached to a household's descendants. The uncertainty of both cases is incisively demonstrated by the authors. Extensive simulations proceeding under a variety of assumptions offer some insights beyond the qualitative result in Eq. (8) about the order of magnitude of tax effects on real consumption.

The issue addressed by Barsky, Mankiw, and Zeldes was already analyzed by Chan (1983). The detailed formulation differs slightly, but the conclusion is the same once the preference structure is properly restricted. Chan emphasizes, however, that the insurance scheme introduced with the special tax policy arrangement is essentially independent of the debt–tax mix problem.

The infinite intertemporal budget constraint of government also reflects a crucial link suspending relevant risks and uncertainty. The equality of present values of expenditures and taxes expresses agents' certain knowledge that current expenditures will eventually be covered by taxation. Suppose, however, that large debt-financed deficits persist for 10, 100, or 1000 years. Is it reasonable to assume an invariant certainty that after $x + 1$ years all will be unwound with appropriately increasing tax liabilities? The basic thrust of rational expectations would suggest that agents learn. An experience of accumulating debt-financed deficits would induce doubts and reservations about the relevance of infinite intertemporal budget constraints. The time-inconsistency problem diligently discussed with examples from tax and monetary policies should actually be highly significant in this context (Baltensperger 1984). Suppose that agents were exposed to a long series of deficits financed by issues of interest-bearing debt. This experience induces some revisions in agents' expectations. The probability assigned to possible defaults, particularly to default by inflation, will rise under the circumstances. The increasing risk associated with large and persistent deficits generates over time an anticipated purchasing-power risk attached to the government debt. This purchasing-power risk modifies the Fisher equation with the appearance of a specific covariance expression representing the purchasing-power risk.

The emergence of this risk term implies an increase both of the nominal and the real rates of interest (Baghat and Wakeman 1983). This problem will be reconsidered in a subsequent section attending to the long-run interdependence of monetary and fiscal policies, an issue raised by Sargent and Wallace (1982).

3.2.d. The changing nature of the issue. The risk problem introduced in the previous paragraph bears essentially on long-run aspects associated with the cumulative effects of a long series of large deficits that erode the relevance of the infinite intertemporal budget constraint expressed in terms of ordinary taxes. This seems to be not the only aspect of risk and uncertainty associated with the macroeconomic consequences of the government's budgetary process. Such risk and uncertainty have so far not been integrated into macroeconomic analysis. Our most recent fiscal experiences suggest that a potentially useful research program would examine the impact of the uncertain amount and nature of tax liabilities on the public's balance-sheet risks and consequently on asset markets, with further effects on consumption and investment. This investigation moves us substantially away from the "Ricardian theme." This theme, restrained by the assumption of lump-sum taxes in order to isolate a possibly pure public-debt effect, can only admit uncertainty about the temporal distribution, the personal incidence of tax liabilities and future income. The first type of uncertainty does not modify the Ricardian theme, but the second and third violate the neutrality pattern of debt-financed deficits. Risk and uncertainty surrounding tax liabilities have a much wider field of operation once we introduce "non-lump-sum" taxes. The uncertain incidence of future tax liabilities on nonhuman wealth, human wealth, and consumption probably affects portfolio risks and thus the required average return. The consequent adjustment in asset values modifies consumption, saving and investment patterns. The importance of debt-financed deficits may, in this context, not so much emerge because of a *direct* effect of public debt on real interest rates in defiance of any "Ricardian equivalence." The deficits and the resulting increase in public debt yield possibly their most important effects via a different channel. These phenomena may be a signal of mounting uncertainty about future magnitude and incidence of tax liabilities. Agents' perceptions bearing on the interpretation of observed deficits would operate as a crucial link in the process. Balance-sheet risks and asset-market responses will vary with the perceived duration of the deficit.

This theme also offers an avenue for an analysis of fiscal *regimes* in contrast to the usual analysis of fiscal policy *actions* and their effects on the evolution of economic activity. Fiscal regimes could be differentiated according to their respective risk patterns parameterized in a specific mode. The procedure would follow the imaginative attempt made by

Stulz and Wasserfallen (1985) for the case of monetary regimes. The investigation was motivated by the recognition of the comparative importance of the stochastic trend and the relatively modest significance of the stationary component in economic fluctuations (Nelson and Plosser 1982). The array of *specific* policy *actions* addressed to the *cyclic* component remains, under the circumstances, confined to a smallish range of influence. Stulz and Wasserfallen show that, in contrast to influences exerted by specific actions, the influence of the *regime's* characteristics expressed by some risk parameters substantially contribute to global economic evolution by conditioning the properties of the stochastic trend. The uncertainty imposed by the regime affects the stochastic properties of assets, their risks, and the portfolio risk with consequences on returns and output behavior. These issues seem worthy of further exploration in a program designed to integrate finance and macroeconomic analysis (Lucas 1984; Plosser 1984; Fischer and Merton 1984).

3.2.e. Some final remarks on the Ricardian theme. It is interesting to reflect at this stage on the consequences of the discussion initiated with Barro's revival of the Ricardian theme. The neoclassic analysis rejects the "conventional" position that the government's financial decisions expressed by the debt–tax mix induce real consequences over both the short and long runs. The IS/LM framework concentrated on the wealth effects of debt policies as the crucial condition of real effects. The Brunner–Meltzer asset-market analysis, on the other hand, emphasized the comparative small order of wealth effects associated with a pure-debt policy even when future tax liabilities were disregarded. The wealth effect measured as the vertical shift elasticity of the pseudodemand line in figure 3.1 occurs as a product of two terms. One term consists of components with opposite signs reflecting offsetting influences produced by interacting asset-markets. The other term is the ratio of government debt at market value to total nonhuman wealth. The real consequences of debt policies in the Brunner–Meltzer asset-market analysis were dominantly produced by substitution and relative price effects produced by the shifting composition of assets. The discussion of the stability analysis revealed furthermore that this short-run, pure-debt effect, again evaluated by shifts of the pseudodemand line, is at best very modest with respect to aggregate output and the price level. This portion of "conventional" analysis assigned more significance to the long-run effects of a pure-debt policy centered on the adjustment of the optimal stock of real capital and consequently the position of the normal output line in Figure 3.1. Both mechanisms stressed by conventional analysis became suspended in the neoclassic analysis. Intergenerational altruism and optimal hedging removed both wealth and substitution effects.

The discussion seems hardly to restore the "conventional" position. Its most significant elements modifying the Ricardian theme do not suggest much potent effects of debt–tax mix policies per se. Kotlikoff's analysis directs our attention neither to any wealth nor subsitution effects. This analysis implies, based on the assumption of "intergenerational selfishness," that debt policies induce intergenerational wealth transfer that modify current real assumption. Debt policy is, however, not a necessary condition of such transfers. Such transfers may occur without debt policy as a result of nontemporal tax shifts. But debt policies do induce, on the other hand, the transfers described by Kotlikoff. This analysis thus emphasizes the effect of debt policies on the composition of aggregate real demand. Debt policies raise real consumption and lower real investment in the short run and lower (comparatively) the capital stock and normal output in the long run. But the mechanism involved differs from those described by conventional analysis. We note, however, that Kotlikoff's analysis is consistent with the operation of a wealth and substitution effect (via asset markets) induced by debt policy.

The consequences of risk and uncertainty induced by debt–financed deficits, so clearly visible in the past five years, may also trace potentially important transmission channels for debt policies. The papers by Baltensperger and Chan are somewhat suggestive in this respect. The issue raised by Baltensperger suggests that an increasing risk of default by inflation associated with a permanent, large, debt-financed deficit raises the purchasing-power risk of government debt and consequently raises the (gross) real of interest. An alternative mode of approaching the same issue proceeds along lines suggested by Bomhoff (1983), Mascaro and Meltzer (1983), and Evans (1984). Permanent and large debt-financed deficits contribute to uncertainty about the course of monetary policy. This uncertainty produces a risk premium embedded in interest rates and raises real rates. And once we move beyond the realm of pure-debt policies and consider deficit policies in a world of distortionary taxes, the risk problem appears, on a first impression, to magnify. But we still lack at this stage an adequate analysis of portfolio risks induced by persistent deficits and the associated uncertain course of tax policies. This analysis would also extend to the effects of such portfolio risks on real consumption, investment, and real returns of assets. We may ultimately learn from the work initiated by the "Ricardian discussion" that the "Ricardian world" offers similar to the Modigliani–Miller theorem a useful benchmark for any analysis of our real problems. It may well be that the new analysis gradually emerging yields insights into more significant mechanisms associated with debt-financed deficits than elaborated by "conventional analysis."

3.3. Some recent empirical work on the Ricardian theme

Analytic arguments and counterarguments hardly settle the issue. They may establish some presumptions with varying weights. An uncertain incidence of future tax liabilities seems to be, for instance, a better approximation to reality than the matching of the distributions of current tax cuts and future tax liabilities. The fact of uncertainty appears clearly more acceptable than its denial or the postulated perfect matching. The approximate realization of such matching in the tax cuts effected on the basis of the Kennedy or Reagan decisions would be, in my judgment, quite astonishing. The matching would have to be reflected in a corresponding matching of experienced tax reductions, additional savings, and resulting acquisitions of government bonds. Simple institutional facts (size of denomination relative to tax cut, access costs to capital markets) distort the pattern and most likely prevent an approximate matching between tax cuts and bond acquisitions, even with a maintained matching between tax cuts and savings. But the partial distortion of the matching need not be decisive per se. The nonmatching segment of taxpayers may be concentrated toward the lower end of the income distribution involving a smallish fraction of total tax cuts. Alternatively, these taxpayers may invest the accrued savings in one form or another of indirect claims on bonds. The financial intermediation involved in this case usually redistributes risk between the intermediary and the holder of its liabilities. The more or less indirect claims on bonds are thus not equivalent to bonds. A positive but smallish wealth effect could thus emerge. But an empirical assessment of the Ricardian thesis along these lines seems very costly and quite uncertain.

A study of another major implication bearing on bequest patterns may be more promising. The Ricardian theme implies that any tax cut relative to permanent government expenditures induces adjustments of bequest by the older generations in order to maintain the utility level of the subsequent generation. A similar effect occurs with changes in social security benefits (i.e., negative taxes) for the older generation. The studies actually executed so far (Feldstein 1978; Barro 1978) yielded conflicting results. A direct examination of bequest patterns linked to major tax-policy shifts could add some information. The Ricardian theme implies, however, in the context of our actual age distribution and conditional life expectation a somewhat loose relation between relative tax cuts and additional bequest. Some of the anticipated tax liabilities will still be borne by the "older" agents. A tighter relation should prevail between relative tax cuts and additional savings, however.

Assessments based on some of the crucial linkages emphasized by the Ricardian hypothesis require a large amount of rather specific information in order to produce approximately useful results. The operation of liquidity constraints offers a good example. There is good evidence for the relevant occurrence of such constraints for some segment under the wealth distribution. We know from various studies that there exist social groups which confront borrowing rates massively higher than the government's borrowing rates. But it is difficult and somewhat speculative to assess the relative significance of this fact without detailed additional cross-sectional data. Professional research quite sensibly attemped, under the circumstances, another route. Early investigations by Tanner (1970) and Kochin (1974) explored the implication bearing on the invariance of consumption expenditures with respect to government debt or debt-financed deficits. Buiter and Tobin (1978), among others, followed these efforts. The net result of this early round was hardly conclusive, with some diversity of results. Six more recent studies by Feldstein (1982), Kormendi (1983), Aschauer (1985), Plosser (1982), Boskin and Kotlikoff (1985) and Bernheim, Shleifer, and Summers (1985) are selected for closer examination.

3.3.a. Feldstein. Feldstein expresses the major implication of the Ricardian thesis in terms of specific constraints on the coefficients in a regression. This regression relates consumers' expenditures (C)

$$C = \beta_0 + \beta_1 Y + \beta_2 W + \beta_3 SSW + \beta_4 G + \beta_5 T$$
$$+ \beta_6 TR + \beta_7 D + \mu \tag{9}$$

with the relevant variables under consideration, where Y is national income, W wealth, SSW measures social security wealth, G expresses government expenditures, T taxes, TR transfer payments, D total government debt, and μ is a random term. All variables are measured in real terms per capita. The Ricardian hypothesis implies the following patterns:

$$\beta_5 = 0, \quad \beta_6 = 0, \quad \beta_3 = 0 \quad \text{and} \quad \beta_7 = -\beta_2.$$

The last condition assures that an increase in measured wealth due to government debt exerts no effect on real consumption. Feldstein considers, in addition, a special "fiscal impotence" hypothesis defined by the four conditions listed plus $\beta_4 = -1$. This hypothesis does not, however, represent the neoclassical position developed specifically by Barro. This problem will be discussed in a subsequent section. The rejection of $\beta_4 = -1$ yields, in particular, no evidence bearing on the Ricardian thesis.

Feldstein concludes an examination of 11 distinct estimations of the regression equation with the judgment that government spending and taxes "can have substantial effects on aggregate demand." He also concludes that "each of the implications of the pre-Ricardian equivalence hypothesis is contradicted by the data." This strong and unambiguous conclusion is somewhat puzzling when evaluated against the results obtained from the regression analysis. The reader may judge for himself with the aid of the following table. This table compares the frequency among the regression results with which the standard error of the coefficient estimate *se* exceeds or equals the coefficient estimate of *ce*, and the number of cases with a coefficient estimate at least double the coresponding standard error.

	$se > ce$	$ce > 2se$
β_5	7	2
β_6		7
β_3	10	

The last condition—that is, $\beta_7 = -\beta_2$—can only be judged on the basis of three regressions. Two cases confirm the hypothesis, and one case provides negative evidence. This pattern is really rather mixed and hardly offers a decisive rejection of the Ricardian thesis. The condition on transfer payments (i.e., $\beta_6 = 0$) emerges as the clearest, but not particularly overwhelming, rejection. The other results bearing on the remaining three conditions seem actually more supportive with respect to the Ricardian thesis.

Several issues associated with the regression analysis obscure the interpretations and assessment of the results. The taxes used naturally refer to "non-lump-sum" taxes with their specific incentives and disincentives. Even a highly significant $\beta_5 < 0$ would be difficult to interpret under the circumstances. We also note that the error-structure problem explored by Plosser and Schwert and the issues associated with potential nonstationarity are neglected.

3.3.b Kormendi. Kormendi recently offered an interesting paper exploring our subject. His discussion expands the role of government following the suggestions of Martin Bailey. The government sector is essentially recognized as a production sector supplying consumption and investment goods. It also operates with a "dissipation factor" representing the social cost of government production. A "consolidated explanation" of private-sector real consumption (excluding purchases of consumer durables) is developed according to the rationality concept of the neoclassical position. This means that households' information about their available resources or opportunities fully reflects the underlying social reality without any distortion of their perceptions. The resulting consumption function is represented by the regression

$$PC_t = a_c + a_{11}Y_t + a_{12}Y_{t-1} + a_2GS_t + a_3W_t + a_4TR_t + u_t, \quad (10)$$

where PC = personal consumption, Y = net national product, GS = government spending on goods and services, W = private real wealth, and TR = transfer payments. All variables are again in real terms. The "consolidated hypothesis" implies that $a_{11} > 0 < a_3$ and $-1 < a_2 < 0$. The magnitude of the latter coefficient reveals the nature of the government sector's production process and of its output. Kormendi emphasizes, moreover, that $a_4 > 0$ can be reconciled with the consolidated hypothesis. This pattern occurs in case transfer payments involve a redistribution from social groups with lower marginal propensity to groups with higher marginal propensity to consume.

The comparative robustness of the "consolidated explanation" yields, in Kormendi's judgment, some initial indications of the neoclassical hypothesis. This robustness is evaluated in accordance with the procedure developed by Plosser and Schwert (1978). The results are quite satisfactory. The estimates derived from the application of ordinary least squares to level data, from generalized least squares, and from first differences coincide very closely.

A second step of the examination enlarges the regression. This yields a "nested specification" subsuming both the standard version and the consolidated explanation:

$$\Delta PC_t = a_0 + a_{11}\Delta Y_t + a_{12}\Delta Y_{t-1} + a_2\Delta GS_t \qquad (11)$$

$$+ a_3\Delta W_t + a_4\Delta TR_t + a_5\Delta TX_t + a_6\Delta RE_t + a_7\Delta GINT + u_t,$$

where TX = taxes, RE = retained earnings, and $GINT$ = interest payments made by the government. The alternative hypotheses imply the following patterns with respect to the crucial four coefficients:

standard version:　　　$a_2 = 0, \quad a_5 < 0, \quad a_6 < 0, \quad a_7 > 0,$
consolidated version:　　$a_2 < 0, \quad a_5 = a_6 = a_7 = 0.$

The results are quite unambiguous. The standard version is clearly rejected. The estimates of a_5, a_6, and a_7 do not differ significantly from zero at standard levels. An F-test applied to the last three coefficients confirms the consolidated version. It should also be noted that the estimates of a_{11}, a_{12}, a_2, a_3, and a_4 coincide with the estimates obtained from the examination of comparative robustness. The standard version implies, moreover, that $a_5 = -a_1 = (a_{11} + a_{12})$. This condition is also rejected.

The test of the net wealth position of government debt yields, in view of the discussion of uncertain future tax liabilities, a remarkably interesting result. The full discounting of future tax liabilities associated with current debt finance implies that the coefficient for government debt D in an extended regression including this variable must be zero. The standard version would assign, in contrast, a positive coefficient. Estimation based on a sample including the war years produces a highly significant *negative* value for the debt coefficient. The exclusion of the war years still yields a *negative* coefficient 1.6 standard errors from zero. The author's interpretation of the result is worth quoting:

> The real income stream deriving from government debt involves inflation risk and some default risk to holders of the debt. The future tax stream implied by the debt, on the other hand, involves that same inflation and default risk plus considerable additional risk as to both its intertemporal and cross-sectional incidence. Thus, in rationally assessing the future tax consequences of government debt, the current certainty equivalent value of the future taxes may exceed the current certainty equivalent value of the income stream (which is simply the market value of the debt). In such a case, the net wealth of the private sector is adversely affected by government debt, implying a negative effect for ΔGB, (and a positive effect for ΔTX) on private consumption.

3.3.c. Aschauer. Aschauer's exploration also addresses, similarly to Feldstein and Kormendi, the implications of the neoclassical thesis bearing on households' consumption behavior. The present paper develops, however, a difference procedure. The author investigates the Ricardian equivalence proposition in the context of an intertemporal optimization framework. A rather standard separable utility function is maximized subject to a consolidated condition derived from combining the representative households and the government's budget constraint. The integrated constraint reflects the households' full recognition of the real conditions determined by the government's fiscal operation. The argument of the utility function refers to "effective consumption" $C^* = C + \Theta G$, defined as the sum of private-sector consumption plus a component of government spending G that contribute to the households' consumption. The parameter Θ expresses the marginal rate of substitution between the two components in effective consumption. With a quadratic utility function, constraint maximization yields an Euler equation

$$EC_t^* = \alpha + \beta C_{t-1}^* . \tag{12}$$

The coefficients are determined by the parameters of the utility function and the constraint. Upon translation into a stochastic context, the Euler equation coincides with Hall's (1981) formulation. The latter argued that in the context of a life cycle model, $\beta = 1$ and that consumption moves along a random walk.

Aschauer supplements the Euler equation with past values of the deficit D and estimates the regression

$$C_t = \alpha + \beta C_{t-1} + \gamma_1 D_{t-1} + \gamma_2 D_{t-2} + \gamma_3 D_{t-3} + \gamma_4 D_{t-4} + \mu_t. \tag{13}$$

This extension was motivated by the author's concern to evaluate the impact of fiscal policy. The neoclassical position incorporated in the underlying optimization schemes implies that all the γ-coefficients are zero. An OLS estimation of the augmented regression yields a clear contradiction of the neoclassical thesis. The deficit variable contributes significantly to the explanation of private consumption C. The sign pattern is significantly different from zero. Aschauer argues that this result "may be more apparent than real due to the fact that past taxes and deficits may help to predict current government spending." This information content of past deficits combined with the substitution relation between G and C conditions nonzero levels for the γ-coefficients.

The author develops this idea in two steps. First he decomposes effective consumption C^* in the (stochastic) Euler equation $EC^* = \alpha + \beta C_{t-1}$ and obtains

$$C_t = \alpha + \beta C_{t-1} + \beta \Theta G_{t-1} - \Theta G_t^0 + u_t, \tag{14}$$

where $G_t^0 = E_{t-1} G_t$. Secondly, he introduces a forecasting equation for G_t in order to relate G_t^0 with observations:

$$G_t = \gamma + \epsilon(L) G_{t-1} + w(L) D_{t-1} + v_t. \tag{15}$$

The last two expressions determine the system with the crucial properties to be estimated and evaluated. This system consists of the forecasting equation, Eq. (15), and Eq. (16):

$$C_t = \delta + \beta C_{t-1} + \eta(L) G_{t-1} + \mu(L) D_{t-1} + u_t. \tag{16}$$

The derivation of the system implies some cross relations linking η with μ and w. These cross relations offer the relevant test statements:

(They) restrict the way in which past government expenditures and past government deficits may influence present consumption expenditure. In particular, if the Ricardian equivalence proposition does not hold, past values of the government deficit should have explanatory power for consumption expenditure apart from the role in forecasting government spending. Consequently, a finding that the data do not do violence (to the restrictions) yields some grounds on which to argue that to a first approximation, the joint assumption of rational expectations and Ricardian equivalence provides a plausible description.

The nature of the formulated hypothesis implies that the relation between constrained and unconstrained estimates determines the crucial test information. The log-likelihood ratio provides thus the relevant test statistic.

It appears that the null hypothesis representing the neoclassical thesis cannot be rejected at a significance level lower than 24 percent. A test based on a forecasting equation for G with longer lags yields a significance level of 10 percent and another test imposing additional constraints shows a significance level of 25 percent for the likelihood statistic.

3.3.d. Provisional comments. Kormendi and Aschauer manage to demonstrate that the neoclassical position represented by the Ricardian equivalence proposition cannot be so easily dismissed. The case for the conventional alternative, which assigns significance to financial decisions, is neither clear nor overwhelming. The evaluation centered on the patterns exhibited by consumption behavior so far remains unsettled and open. Advocates of the "conventional hypothesis" (like the author of this paper) are forced to admit that the neoclassical position deserves serious investigation. Further examination may affect both the conventional and the neoclassical thesis. Neither position may survive unscathed. The suggestions concerning the role of uncertainty and risk joined with Kormendi's estimate of the debt parameter may give a clue for possible future work. Such work should, in particular, also attend to a serious gap in the papers discussed above. The Ricardian proposition implies a tight relation between relative tax cuts, additional savings and acquisitions of government debt by households. According to this proposition the induced additional savings do not spill over beyond bond acquisition to consumer durables. The absence of any significant effect of the relevant fiscal policy variables on real consumption expressed by nondurables, services, and use-value of durables offers only very partial evidence. The regressions explored need be complemented with a similar regression addressed to the investment in consumer durables and possibly other assets typically held by households that are not equivalent to government debt.

Some problems associated with Aschauer's paper need to be noted. The statistical work is based on level data. The error structure problem emphasized by Plosser and Schwert may not be serious according to the value of the DW statistic. The problem posed by potentially nonstationary data remains and is not clear in its implications. Some more attention, as exemplified by Kormendi, to these troublesome issues would seem desirable. Aschauer's procedure offers, moreover, no sharply focused discriminating test between the neoclassical and the alternative thesis. The Euler equation supplemented with lagged deficits [i.e., Eq. (13)] hardly represents the "conventional thesis." The weird pattern of coefficients for D_{t-1} and D_{t-2} contradicts the conventional thesis. The subsequent test based on Eq. (15) and (16) with their cross parameter properties thus offers at best a test of the neoclassical proposition against an uninterpreted class represented by the augmented Euler equation *excluding* the conventional thesis.

3.3.e. Plosser. Plosser's examination of the Ricardian thesis addresses an entirely different dimension than the previous three papers. His paper investigates the implication of the Ricardian hypothesis bearing on asset-market patterns. A temporal reallocation of taxes expressed by a corresponding accumulation or decumulation of debt does not affect asset prices and interest rates under the Ricardian hypothesis. The basic idea is implemented in the spirit of a neoclassic analysis. Market efficiency or rational expectation is combined with the expectations hypothesis of the term structure of interest rates. This analytic foundation implies a relation between the surprises in holding period yields of securities with different maturities and corresponding surprises in fiscal or monetary magnitudes:

$$H_{t+1} - EH_{t+1} = B[X_{t+1} - EX_{t+1}] + v_{t+1},$$

where H_{t+1} is a column vector of holding period returns from t to $t + 1$ of bonds of various maturities, E refers to the expectational magnitude, B is a matrix conformable with the dimensions of the vectors H and X; the latter vector contains the relevant fiscal and monetary variables. These variables refer in this specific case to the debt monetized by the central bank—the government debt held by the public and government purchases of goods and services. v_{t+1} denotes a random vector.

The neoclassical position implies that an unexpected increase in government purchases raises interest rates and thus lowers holding period returns. This implication is compatible with Keynesian or monetarist analysis. The underlying analysis, however, attributes the result in each case to a somewhat different mechanism. The crucial difference between the neoclassical thesis and the alternative positions, however, surrounds the role of government debt. Surprises in this magnitude yield no consequences with respect to holding period returns under the Ricardian hypothesis. They should produce, in contrast, negatively related consequences under the alternative hypotheses. Lastly, surprises in the monetized portion of the public debt yield, according to Keynesian and (older) monetarist analysis, positively related surprises in holding period returns. Neoclassical analysis is not inherently inconsistent with a nonvanishing effect of monetary surprises. It remains, however, somewhat ambiguous on this point without further specifications bearing on expectations and shock structure. With some dominance of comparatively permanent shocks in the monetary variable, its surprises convey a useful signal value bearing on future inflation. This response mechanism would produce *negative* reactions in holding period returns to *positive* monetary surprises. These reactions would, moreover, increase with the maturity of the security under consideration.

In order to complete the analysis, two analytic building blocks are added. The forecasting equation

$$X_{t+1} = A(L)X_t + u_{t+1} \tag{17}$$

is introduced with $A(L)$ designating a matrix of polynomials in the lag operator L; u again refers to a random vector. This formulation advances implicitly an hypothesis about the structure of the process generating the observations of the X-vector. Lastly, an expression for EH_{t+1} is derived from the rational expectation theory of the term structure:

$$EH_{t+1} = R_{1t} + \phi ,$$

where R_{1t} refers to a vector consisting only of the current one-period spot rate, and ϕ is a vector containing the marginal increments of liquidity premia associated with different maturities beyond the spot rate. Plosser also offers an alternative interpretation of ϕ based on the Sharp–Lintner capital-asset model. In this case ϕ would be equal to a β-vector multiplied by the difference between the expectation of a holding period yield for a market basket and the certain current spot rate R_{1t}.

The first step in the empirical examination evaluates the joint hypothesis about market efficiency and the term structure. The implication that current surprises of holding period returns are independent of past observations on money, debt, and government purchases is tested with a suitable regression. The results are quite unambiguous and support the joint hypothesis. A second step in the procedure explores the statistical results bearing on the matrix of coefficients B in Eq. (16). Holding period returns for four different maturities are investigated. In two cases the coefficient estimate of the debt variable is less than its standard error. One coefficient estimate is significant at the 10 percent level, and the fourth coefficient estimate, slightly exceeding its standard error, occurs with a significance level above 10 percent. All coefficient estimates associated with the debt variable are positive. The signs are thus inconsistent with the "conventional analysis." The significance levels confirm, on the other hand, the null hypothesis expressed by the neoclassic thesis. Sign and significance level together yield a clear rejection of the "conventional hypothesis."

The coefficient estimates of the monetary variable also support some version of the neoclassic thesis. Their signs, with the exception of the security with the shortest maturity, are, however, consistent with the "conventional analysis." Only one out of four coefficients reaches a significance level of at most 10 percent. The sign and the confirmation of the null hypothesis obviously provide no support for the supplementary hypothesis bearing on the signal effect of monetary surprises in the context of a specific shock structure mentioned above. The coefficient estimates associated with government purchases provide some support for the occurrence of an effect. All estimates exhibit the sign implied by the hypothesis. Two of the four estimates are significant at the 5 percent level and one at the 10 percent level. The significance level for holding period returns on the longest maturity rises beyond 10 percent. We also note the significant estimates for the constant parameter in the regression. This confirms the occurrence of a liquidity premium or the operation of a non-vanishing β-factor on government securities.

The interpretation of the test deserves some attention. This issue may be usefully addressed with the aid of a somewhat more explicit characterization of the test procedure. The following pair of propositions control the test:

$$F \supset [ME \cdot EHTS \cdot NCH \supset T], \quad F \supset [ME \cdot EHTS \cdot CH \supset -T].$$

F refers to a sentence presenting the hypothesis summarized in the forecasting equation; ME denotes a sentence advancing the market efficiency hypothesis, and $EHTS$ denotes a hypothesis about the term structure of interest rates; NCH and CH refer to the alternative hypothesis—that is, the neoclassical and the conventional. Lastly, T refers to the test statement about the B coefficients under the null hypothesis. The crucial point to be addressed here is the conditionality of the test relative to the untested hypothesis contained in F. The compelling force of any confirmation or disconfirmation of T depends decisively on the assumption made about F. Suppose F is true and $ME \cdot EHTS$ and T are confirmed. We can effectively discriminate under the circumstances and conclude that NCH is confirmed and CH disconfirmed. But suppose that F is false. The logical relations between the various sentences offer in this case no grounds to discriminate between NCH and CH on the basis of tests bearing on T. With the truth of F given, and $ME \cdot EHTS$ confirmed independently, the confirmation of T *must* disconfirm CH and *can* confirm NCH in order to satisfy the truth of the whole conditional proposition. Should F, on the other hand, be false, then the whole conditional is true irrespective of our decision about NCH, CH, and T. The truth of the conditional imposes under the circumstances no constraint on confirmation or disconfirmation of NCH or CH relative to any given decision about T. The falsehood of F implies that the test is irrelevant and uninformative. It follows that in the absence of any information about F the results of the test cannot be assigned substantial weight.

One procedure designed to raise the informativeness of the test involves repetition with a variety of different forecasting equations. Plosser's paper moves in this direction. The test is repeated with a forecasting equation including current bond-market information. The results bearing on government purchases appear somewhat sharpened. The other results are essentially unchanged. We may conclude that Plosser's paper does not essentially modify the balance of evidence summarized above. It did, however, usefully direct our attention to an alternative dimension—the financial markets and the corresponding opportunities for systematic future examinations of the neoclassic thesis.

3.3.f. Bernheim–Shleifer–Summers and Boskin–Kotlikoff. Two papers recently appeared in the professional circuit that appear to shift the balance of evidence somewhat against the hypothesis of debt neutrality. Both papers move beyond the macro data applied to an examination of consumers' behavior. They exploit in very different ways some micropatterns systematically related to the relevant analysis. The first paper, by Bernheim, Shleifer, and Summers (1985), seems particularly noteworthy. It starts with the observation that most of the existing wealth was transmitted by the prior generation. We noted in a previous paragraph that an "accidental transfer" hypothesis without any bequest motive could explain the *occurrence* of bequests in a non-Ricardian world. This explanation would probably hold even with an availability of annuities. But it seems doubtful that this hypothesis can explain the order of magnitude of the bequests. The crucial contribution made by BSS (i.e., the three authors) emerges from the explicit construction of a detailed ("non-Ricardian") hypothesis explaining the occurrence of bequests that incorporates a bequest motive. This hypothesis, in spite of the acknowledged bequest motive, yields radically different implications from Barro's hypothesis. The explicit specification of this alternative bequest hypothesis offers opportunities for new and richer critical evaluations with untapped data.

The "exchange motivated bequests" hypothesis involves a simple idea developed with a subtle analysis. The idea applies the basic REMM (resourceful, evaluating, maximizing man) model to the interactions between older and younger persons. The hypothesis thus rejects Barro's assumption that older persons are concerned about the future consumption opportunities of their descendants. Older generations accumulate wealth in tradeable (i.e., bequeathable) form in order to purchase services from the younger generation. The services bought by the prospect of bequests occur essentially in the form of attention extended by the younger to the older. An implicit exchange transaction of potential wealth for current attention determines the evenutal wealth transfer from older to younger.

The authors structure their analysis with two sets of utility functions and a set of constraints describing wealth accumulations over time. The utility functions represent the agents in the interacting groups. The expression

$$\sum_{t=S}^{\infty} \beta^{t-s} P(\epsilon, t) U_t(C_t, a_t) \tag{18}$$

describes the utility function of the testator, where β is a discount factor, $P(s,t)$ is the probability of survival from the initial period s to period t and U_t is the instantaneous utility as a function of consumption C_t and the attention vector $a_t = (a_{1t} \cdots a_{nt})$. This attention vector describes the degree of attention extended to the testator by each of the N members of the set A of "credible" beneficiaries addressed by the testator. The latter's utility increases with C_t and a_t. He is also assumed to have a finite deterministic life span T so that $P(s, T + 1) = 0$.

The utility function of the N beneficiaries is given by

$$\sum_{t=s}^{\infty} \beta_n^{t-s} U_{nt}(C_n, a_{nt}). \tag{19}$$

We need only comment here that BSS assume beneficiaries to live forever. This assumption simplifies matters with no loss in relevant substance. U_n has a positive derivative with respect to $C_{n,t}$ and a negative derivative with respect to $a_{n,t}$. Attention is valued quite differently by the two sides of the exchange.

Expressions (20) and (21) introduce descriptions of wealth accumulations.

a. $\quad w_{t+1} = (W_t - C_t - A_t)(1 + r_t) + A_t(1 + \rho_t), \tag{20}$

b. $\quad B_t = W_t - C_t - A_t.$

The first applies to testators, with W designating wealth, A the annuity investment made, r the market rate of interest, ρ_t the rate of return on A, and $B = \sum_n b_n$ the total sum of bequests; b_n is the component of B going to beneficiary n. Formulation (a) holders in case the testator survives, and (b) holds in the case of death during the period.

$$W_{n,t=1} = (W_{n,t} - C_t + b_{n,t}I(t - 1))(1 + r_t). \tag{21}$$

Expression (21) supplies the condition for beneficiary n. $I(t) = 1$ in case the testator dies during the period; otherwise it is zero.

The structure of the strategy game between testators and beneficiaries has now been defined. The testator invests in bequeathable wealth in order to induce attention from potential beneficiaries, and the latter compete with attention for bequests. BSS develop a clever and intricate argument to determine a (Nash) solution to this game. A general sense of the detailed argument will suffice here. The testator chooses an optimal plan $(C, a, b_1^*, \ldots, b_N)$ for consumption, attention, level, and distribution of bequests. Optimization proceeds subject to the constraints, including a feasibility condition. The latter imposes that the choice of $(a, b_1, \ldots, b_N)$ must be confined to a range assuring to beneficiaries at least a utility equal to nonparticipation in the game (i.e., $a_n = b_n = 0$). The beneficiaries may be interpreted to play a subgame conditioned on the vector $(b_1^*, \ldots, b_N^*)$. The testator can, of course, not impose his optimal choice of attention on beneficiaries. He thus faces a problem of selecting a bequest rule—that is, a vector function $b(H,B)$, where H denotes the history of the game and B the total level of bequests—that induces beneficiaries to supply a^* voluntarily in their own interests. BSS show the existence of a specific rule in situations with at least two beneficiaries. This rule does produce a Nash equilibrium solution (a^*, b^*). This equilibrium implies that the testator fully appropriates the surplus utility created by the exchange. The Ricardian equivalence theorem fails to be satisfied under this "exchange motivated bequests" hypothesis. Bequests do occur and they are motivated. They are, however, not motivated by the future welfare of descendants but by the purchase of current attention. A debt-financed deficit yields, in general, under the circumstances, no offsetting intergenerational transfers and personal saving. Opportunities are modified and real variables change.

An extensive empirical evaluation follows the analytic argument. The hypothesis implies that parents influence their children's behavior by holding wealth in bequeathable forms. It implies, in particular, that contacts between parents and children within families with bequeathable wealth are more extensive. The authors exploit the data from a longitudinal retirement history survey. They especially derive data on bequests b and contacts. A normalized measure V of contacts per child is constructed with the raw data. An OLS regression of V on b yields the "proper sign" but does not confirm the hypothesis. The authors trace this negative result to potential endogeneity of b. The hypothesis does imply that b and V are simultaneously and interactingly determined. A TSLS procedure thus corresponds better to the structure of the hypothesis. The results are dramatically different in this case. The null hypothesis of no effect on b on V can be rejected with high confidence. A special test assessing the exogeneity of b supports the choice of a TSLS procedure. Exogeneity of b can also be rejected with substantial confidence.

The authors recognize that consistency of the empirical pattern with the hypothesis cannot exclude other possible explanations. They evaluate a variety of such alternatives in order to strengthen support for the hypothesis advanced. They consider thus the possibility that influences emanating from several omitted and personal dimensions are erroneously attributed to b. The effect of b on V survives this examination. Some alternative explanations of the observed correlation between V and b do not distinguish between wealth in bequeathable and in nonbequeathable forms. The hypothesis advanced assigns, in contrast, no significance to the latter. The statistical results again confirm the hypothesis under examination. The case for alternative hypotheses emphasizing the role of the cost of contacts imposed on children or of the parents housing wealth fails similarly when confronted with relevant data. Other implications are also exploited in order to extend the range of relevant observations bearing on the hypothesis. Lastly, data on the comparatively low frequency of privately purchased annuities or of gifts offer some useful information. BSS discriminate, with their help, between the hypothesis considered, the "accidental bequest" hypothesis discussed in a previous section, the "bequests for their own sake" hypothesis, and the "intergenerational altruism" hypothesis. The authors' hypothesis also survives this last round of assessments. A careful reader of this paper may agree that the wide-ranging and imaginative empirical evaluation establishes a serious case on behalf of the hypothesis that bequests are a component of an exchange. The relevant and pervasive occurrence of such transactions is, moreover, inconsistent with the Ricardian thesis of debt neutrality.

A serious limitation of prior studies bearing on the Ricardian thesis is their concentration on macro data of consumption patterns. BSS substantially enriched our assessment by exploring a wider range of implications requiring micro data. Boskin and Kotlikoff (1985) pursue a similar course in an investigation that required a massive labor and computational input. Their examination addresses an important implication of the Ricardian hypothesis expressed by the intergenerational altruism model. Under this hypothesis consumption expenditures depend only on "collective resources" representing the real underlying situation. It implies, in particular, that consumption does not depend on the age distribution of the population. The analysis is based on a present value of family utility. This formulation involves a series of instantaneous utility functions specified for all descendants and their respective age groups. A description of wealth accumulation for both household and government serves as a constraint on the optimal choice for an intertemporal consumption pattern of the "infinitely living" family. The first-order condition determines an expression within the usual family of Euler equations relating consumption in adjacent periods. The problem, however, allows no tractable analytic solution describing consumption as a function of predetermined magnitudes. The authors thus pursue with great patience a different course. They solve a finite-period approximation to the infinite optimization problem. The approximation is chosen so as to lower changes in the optimal consumption pattern produced by extending the period to a negligible level. The data set used covers the period 1946–81. A dynamic programming approach is applied to compute the solutions for the relevant sample period. It should be noted that this optimal pattern $\bar{C}$ is derived in the context of stochastic uncertainty about future rates of return and earnings. The derivation, moreover, depends on a specific utility function and an age-weight assigned to age-group instantaneous utilities. The authors actually investigate combinations of parameters (of instantaneous utility and the discount factor) in order to find the selection that determines for $\bar{C}$ the closest fit (in terms of root mean squares) to the data.

The test is performed with a regression of actual consumption C on C and five age groups expressed in terms of their respective income shares. They hypothesis of intergenerational altruism,

$$C = \beta_0 + \beta_1 \bar{C} + \lambda_1 s_1 + \cdots \lambda_5 s_5 + \epsilon, \qquad (22)$$

implies that $\lambda_0 = \lambda_i = 0$ for $i = 1, \ldots, 5$ and $\beta_1 = 1$. The statistical inference confirms the last condition but disconfirms the others. The pattern of λ-coefficients seems consistent with some life cycle hypothesis. The coefficient pattern estimated implies, in particular, that a redistribution of 10 percent of income from the younger to the older generation would raise consumption by 1 percent and lower the net national savings rate by 9 percent.

The authors' preliminary capital and labor-intensive investigation clearly disconfirms the Ricardian thesis couched in terms of an "intergenerational altruism" hypothesis. This disconfirmation must be substantially qualified, however. The test does not uniquely address this crucial hypothesis. It is mixed with an array of auxiliary hypotheses bearing on the choice of utility function, age-weight assignments, the specification of uncertainty, and other components. The disconfirmation could, of course, apply to the set of auxiliary hypotheses. This comment does not lower the value of a major piece of work developed by Boskin and Kotlikoff. Their examination does reenforce the results obtained by BSS, and further research involving variations in the choice of auxiliary hypotheses may confirm the rejection of the Ricardian thesis.

3.4. A neoclassical analysis of government expenditures

The Ricardian theme does not imply irrelevance of fiscal policy. Expenditures and taxes remain potent instruments shaping output, employment, and welfare. Barro (1981b, 1984) also initiated in this field the neoclassical explorations. The general analysis of fiscal policy uses the same market-clearing approach so extensively exploited in monetary analysis.

Barro's discussion of fiscal policy moves incisively beyond the sinkhole theory of the government's operations. The private-sector output acquired by the public sector forms the basis for the supply of public consumption goods to households and productive input services to private producers. "Public consumption" competes to some extent with private consumption. A parameter, α, summarizes this fact. It expresses the marginal rate of substitution between public and private consumption. With $\alpha = 1$, "public consumption" and "private consumption" substitute one for one. A vanishing α—that is, $\alpha = 0$—reflects absence of any substitution between the two types of consumption. With $0 < \alpha < 1$ a unit increase in "public consumption" lowers private consumption by less than one unit.

The government's supply of productive services raises an input available to private producers. Private-sector output thus expands in accordance with the marginal productivity of this input in private production. A parameter β reflects this marginal productivity. The parameter describes the increase in private-sector output produced by a unit increase in government real expenditures. Government real expenditures both fully reflect the public sector's absorption of private output and its supply of goods and services to the private sector. The government sector is made to behave as if it contracted for goods and services produced by the private sector that are immediately made available to private households and producers. It is, moreover, assumed that the government's input services do not affect the marginal product of labor and capital in the private production process.

The system used to analyze the impact of government expenditures and (distortionary) taxes is confined to some basic elements expressed by two equations:

$$C(r, G_1, \overline{G},...) + I(r,...) + G_1 = Y(r,G_1, \overline{G},...), \tag{23}$$

$$M = L(r+\pi, Y, G_1,...). \tag{24}$$

Equation (23) describes the market-clearing condition for the output market. The various symbols have standard meanings: C = private real consumption, I = private-sector real investment, G_1 = current government real expenditures, $\overline{G}$ = permanent government real expenditures anticipated for a horizon beyond the current period, Y = real income, r = real rate of interest, M = money stock, P = price level, and π = expected rate of inflation. The signs below the variables indicate the direction of response of the dependent variable. The two distinct magnitudes for government real expenditures are introduced in order to analyze the impact of transitory and permanent changes in government expenditures. This analysis proceeds initially under the assumption of lump-sum taxes. Distortionary taxes are introduced at a later stage. The path of the money stock together with the two government expenditure variables refer to the exogeneous components in the analysis. This implies that π is also held fixed in accordance with the path of M.

We consider first the impact of a transitory increase of G_1. A simple diagram (Figure 3.3) is used for this purpose. Line d represents the demand for output occurring on the left side of Eq. (23). Line s marks the supply located on the right of the same equation. An increase in G_1 against a background of a constant permanent government expenditure implies that some expected future expenditures must fall to offset the temporary rise of G_1. Constancy of $\bar{G}$ means that the representative real opportunities expressing the households real wealth remains unchanged. These real opportunities are defined by the difference between the present value of future real income and the present value of future government real expenditures.

A constant $\bar{G}$ implies that an increase in G_1 induces no wealth effect on demand or supply of output. This means, in particular, that $\Delta G_1 > 0$ shifts the demand and supply line in the graph for reasons other than changes in basic real opportunities. The net effect of the impact on output and real interest rates can be easily determined by comparison of the horizontal shifts of the two curves. The supply shifts to the right by an amount β per unit change in G_1, whereas demand shifts by an amount of

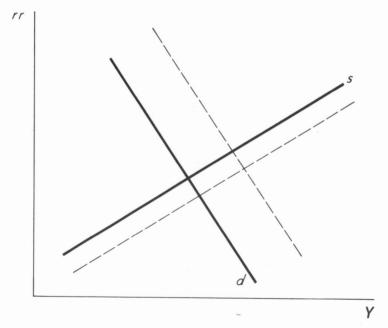

Figure 3.3

$1 - \alpha$ in the same direction. Assuming that $\alpha + \beta < 1$, as Barro does, the increase of G_1 creates an excess demand of $1 - \alpha - \beta$ per unit increase at the initial real rate. The market-clearing condition thus forces a rise in the real rate of interest. The simultaneous shift of both curves to the right assures, moreover, that output also rises. We note immediately that we observe, in contrast to a Keynesian analysis, no multiplier effect. The diagram suggests that the increase in output per unit increase in G_1 is less than $1 - \alpha < 1$. The economy's response thus imposes a crowding-out effect on both private consumption and investment. Crowding out is, however, avoided with $\beta = 1$ and $\alpha = 0$.

The solution for r and Y can be inserted into the portfolio equation in order to determine the response of the price level. Before we consider this final result we need to examine the rationale of G_1 in money demand. G_1 operates in the nature of an in-kind transfer. It is thus interpreted to lower, relative to Y, the household's monetary transactions. The increase in G_1 thus reenforces the effect of a higher real rate of interest on real balances. The net result thus depends on the comparative strength of the income effect. The price level rises in response to a temporary increase in government expenditures, provided that the effect exerted by r and G_1 on real balances dominates the income effect. With a dominant income effect, prices fall.

A different pattern emerges under a permanent increase in government expenditures. This requires a simultaneous rise in G_1 and $\overline{G}$. We need to consider, therefore, the consequences of an increase in $\overline{G}$. Once again we evaluate the shifts in demand and supply of output. We note first that the immediate effects induced by G_1 expressed by α on household demand and β on production do not occur in this case. The increase in $\overline{G}$ with G_1 constant provides no additional goods or services in the current period. The current impact of $\overline{G}$ operates via wealth and labor effort. A unit, increase in $\overline{G}$ lowers real opportunities of the private sector by one unit, holding r constant. This is modified by future α and β effects. The first effect provides additional resources to households, and the second raises the future income stream. Additional modification results from a higher labor supply produced by lower real wealth. This last modification raises real income by an amount a. The net wealth decline is thus $1 - \alpha - \beta - a$. Barro postulates at this stage a one-to-one relation between changes in real wealth and real consumption. This implies that the average propensity to consume with respect to wealth prossesses a suitable positive derivative with respect to real wealth. The increase in $\overline{G}$ induces no direct effects on investment and G_1. The total direct-demand effect coincides therefore with the horizontal shift of the consumption function—that is, $-(1 - \alpha - \beta - a)$. We combine this shift in aggregate demand due to $\overline{G}$ with the shift due to G_1 (which is $1 - \alpha$) and obtain $\beta + a$ as the net shift in aggregate demand attributable to a *permanent* rise in government expenditures. This matches the positive horizontal shift on the supply side, which also equals $\beta + a$. It follows that a permanent expansion of government expenditures raises output with no effect on real rates of interest. The price level effect is algebraically larger than the response produced by a transitory increase in government expenditures. But the price effect still remains ambiguous and conditioned by the comparative strength of Y and G_1 in money demand. The dominance of Y implies a *fall* in the price level. Lastly, similar to the case of transitory expenditure increases, there occurs no multiplier effect. The expansion of output $\beta + a < 1$ is less than the unit increase in $G_1 + \overline{G}$. The resulting crowding out is, moreover, concentrated on private consumption.

The impact of tax policies is investigated in a similar vein. A flat-rate tax on income net of depreciation and exemption is introduced. This tax modifies the relevant margins for household and investor decisions. This modification implies that the after-tax real rate of interest and the tax rate appear as arguments in the consumption and supply functions. It follows that an increase in the tax rate offset by expanded exemptions in order to satisfy the government's budget constraint lowers output and real interest rate.

This analysis has been exposed by Barro to some empirical assessment. One evaluation (1984a) traces the broad contours of transitory expenditures. Such expenditures are essentially confined to war episodes and thus emerge for all practical purposes in the nature of military expenditures. The Vietnam episode can be disregarded, since the comparatively negligible magnitude of transitory spending (2 percent of GNP) is probably swamped by other influences on real GNP. In contrast, the two world wars and the Korean war episode are quite informative. Transitory spending loomed with substantial force. It is remarkable that aggregate output responded with a fraction of around .55 to .60 to transitory expenditures in all three cases. It is noteworthy, moreover, that crowding out operated dominantly on real investment. These observations appear quite consistent with the implication of Barro's analysis.

A more thorough statistical investigation addressed the relation between aggregate output on the one side and both transitory or permanent expenditures on the other side. The latter two variables were represented by some ingeniously complicated measures, which probably avoid nonstationary characteristics. The nonstationary character of output is attended by the inclusion of a time trend. The results seem remarkably consistent with the implications bearing on the response pattern of output. Transitory expenditures induce a larger impact than permanent expenditures. But the case for even a most modest multiplier effect for transitory spending remains quite weak. Still, larger permanent expenditures do lift aggregate output permanently above the time trend, but at some cost of private real expenditures.

The results may be sensitive to the range of auxiliary hypotheses guiding the measurement procedures. Further investigations along this interesting approach need to be explored in order to deepen the assessment of a neoclassical fiscal analysis. One particular issue needs our attention in this context. Nelson and Plosser (1982), followed by Stulz and Wasserfallen (1985), demonstrated with extensive tests that the hypothesis of a deterministic trend is overwhelmingly dominated by the hypothesis of a stochastic trend. A stochastic trend usually collapses the stationary component and radically modifies the results of regression analysis applied to it. One suspects that substituting a stochastic trend for the time trend and then regressing the resulting stationary component on transitory and permanent expenditures would substantially alter the outcome.

Some comments should still be addressed to the analysis. The contrast with Keynesian analysis should be noted first. Barro confirms that an essentially price-theoretical approach (Brunner 1970) lowers the significance of interacting multiplying flows. The latter moves into center stage of the analysis once we proceed on the assumption of given price level or nominal wages. A "non-market-clearing" analysis typically converts fiscal actions into a multiplier effect on output. This effect is produced by variations induced in aggregate demand encountering unresponsive prices. Barro's neoclassical approach differs radically from the Keynesian tradition. Fiscal policy is analyzed in the context of full information and market clearing. This context would prevent any real effects of monetary shocks. This environment does not preclude temporary and permanent real responses to fiscal actions. These responses, however, depend crucially on the properties of output supply. The supply responses fully determine the output effect of permanent expenditure increases. We also note the emphasis on changing output composition produced by fiscal action associated with the "crowding out" of private consumption and investment. The difference in this respect between temporary and permanent fiscal action is also significant. This result cannot be reproduced within the standard IS/LM framework.

There remains a question bearing on the interpretation of this analysis. The full information market-clearing approach describes, in my judgment, a benchmark forming a "gravitational center" of economic processes approximating long-run aspects. Two important revisions would probably move us somewhat closer to reality in some sense without sacrificing Barro's basic price-theoretical thrust. The prevalence of incomplete information needs to be recognized, and a more general concept of market clearing needs to be used. This concept acknowledges that prices do not reflect all ongoing shocks. They will rationally reflect perceived permanent shocks but not (perceived) transitory shocks. There will be a market clearing under the circumstances relative to (perceived) permanent shocks but not with respect to *all* shocks. Some shock-absorbing buffers thus operate in the economy and distribute the output adjustment to shocks over time. This pattern would probably produce a more substantial difference between the effects of temporary and permanent expenditure changes.

A representative work of neoclassical analysis in the new mode was recently developed by Aschauer and Greenwood (1985). The analysis is built in a dynamic choice-theoretic context. A representative household optimizes over two periods subject to a constraint that incorporates tax parameters affecting labor income in either period and a tax parameter imposed on the second period's capital income. Market-clearing conditions are added for each period. These conditions reveal on the supply side the structure of production; that is, investment in the first period adds to output in the second period. The first-order optimality condition together with the market-clearing condition determines the system of equations used to examine the impact of fiscal policy. A budget constraint for the government sector with a "Ricardian thrust" assures a consistent pattern of fiscal action. Moreover, the government provides, similar to Barro's case, consumption goods to households and input services to private producers. The households' utility function depends, moreover, on total consumption available to the household, which is the sum of private consumption and the weighted government contribution with weight less than unity. This weight again represents the marginal rate of substitution between the two types of consumption.

The analytic structure is applied to an examination of tax policies, stabilization policy with the aid of adjustable tax parameters, expenditure policies, and optimal taxation. An increase in the second period's (flat) tax rate on labor income induces intertemporal substitutions that raise the first period's labor supply and investment, but lower the second period's labor supply. The welfare effect of this tax increase depends crucially on the occurrence of distortionary taxes. Welfare falls when first-period income is untaxed. Welfare rises, however, in case first-period income is already taxed. The new tax modifies to some extent the intertemporal distortion of the first tax.

The consequences of stabilization policy are explored under the assumption that the production process in the second period is subjected to random shocks. The larger their variance, the lower the representative households' welfare level. But a stabilization policy operating with a state-contingent tax parameter actually lowers the welfare level. However, uncertainty due to stabilization raises current consumption and decreases current work effort, output, and investment.

A temporary (unexpected) increase in first-period government expenditures (expressed by a linear combination of consumption and productive services) lowers welfare, provided the marginal product of government productive services and the marginal rate of substitution between private and public consumption is less than unity. Work effort in both periods increases, whereas investment declines. Output rises in the first period and falls in the second period.

An anticipated increase in the second-period government expenditures *raises* first-period investment and work effort in both periods. The consequences of a *permanent* increase in government expenditures follow from combining the prior two cases. Work effort and output rise in both periods, and consumption declines.

Aschauer's (1985) elaborate analysis produces results somewhat similar to Barro's investigation. The argument also proceeds on the basis of full information and continuous full-market clearing. There is, however, no money and, thus, no price level in the model. The choice-theoretic foundation prevents simply adding a money demand equation. Money would have to be added to the utility function or embedded in a production or exchange constraint (Brunner 1951). The usual homogeneity conditions can, however, be expected to be satisfied. Aschauer's results probably carry over to a monetary economy. Finally, an examination of the detailed structural knowledge required for stabilization and optimal tax policy reveals the dubious relation between such analysis and actual policy issues. This aspect will be reconsidered in the last section of the paper.

4. Deficits, Monetary Regimes, and Economic Activity

4.1. The endogenous states of the monetary regime: Sargent and Wallace

The "stability problem" associated with deficit finance revealed an interrelation between fiscal and monetary regimes. This issue surfaced again in recent years, but in a modified context. Thomas Sargent and Neil Wallace (1982) approached the interrelation between the two regimes, or the financial coordination problem, with a concern directed to a very different issue. They question the long-run survival of an anti-inflationary monetary regime when confronted with persistent deficits sufficiently large to raise the real stock of government debt relative to real national product. The problem may be explored with the aid of the government's budget constraint:

$$\overset{o}{S} + \overset{o}{B} = G + TR - TA + iS, \tag{25}$$

where S denotes the stock of publicly held debt, B is the monetary base, G refers to nominal government expenditures on goods and services, TR designates transfer payments, and TA designates tax revenues; i should be interpreted as the average interest rate on outstanding debt. The budget equation can be translated into the following expression:

$$\overset{o}{s} = \overline{\text{def}} + \left[(rr - n) + \left[n - \frac{\Delta y}{y} + \left[\pi - \frac{\Delta p}{p} \right] \right] \right] s \tag{26}$$

$$- \left[(\pi + n) + \left[\frac{\Delta p}{p} - \pi \right] + \left[\frac{\Delta y}{y} - n \right] \right] b - \overset{o}{b},$$

where s describes the ratio of real debt to real national income. b similarly represents the volume of base money per unit of nominal national income (i.e., it is the reciprocal of base velocity), $\overline{\text{def}}$ consists of the basic deficit ratio expressed as

$$\overline{\text{def}} = \frac{G + TR - TA}{Y}, \tag{27}$$

with Y indicating nominal national product. The other symbols are $rr =$ real interest rate, $n =$ normal rate of real growth, $y =$ actual output, $\pi =$ expected rate of inflation, and p is the price level.

Expression (26) may be considered as a differential equation in s. A stable process requires that the bracketed expression associated with s on the right side be negative. Actual real growth $\Delta y/y$ and actual inflation $\Delta p/p$ sufficiently large would produce a negative sign. But this state is purely transitory. Over the long run relevant for this investigation the sign would be determined by $rr - n$, the relation between the real rate and the normal growth rate. This relation appeared with a major role in traditional growth theory. It implicitly occurs also in the analysis surrounding infinite intertemporal budget constraints. The arguments bearing on the Ricardian thesis require, in particular, that $rr > n$. A real rate rr exceeding the normal real growth n is a necessary condition for the Ricardian thesis. Government debt would appear as net wealth under the opposite inequality. However, the inequality $rr < n$ raises subtle issues about its relevant occurrence in a steady-state context. A major problem is the reconciliation of finite assets values with $rr \leqslant n$. Such reconciliation could possibly be achieved in a model combining "intergenerational selfishness" with uncertainty of death (Blanchard 1984). This combination would determine a discount rate exceeding the real rate of interest.

The relevant long-run relations may now be written as

$$\overset{o}{s} = \overline{\text{def}} + (rr - n)s - (\pi + n)b. \tag{28}$$

We note that a steady-state condition also requires that $\overset{o}{b} = 0$. This expresses the fact that the price level is fully adjusted at any time to the prevailing volume of the monetary base, and b is fully adjusted to the ongoing inflation. Under the first state—that is, $rr > n$—consistent with the Ricardian thesis, the debt–deficit process is unstable. For any initial value $\overset{o}{s} > 0$ the real debt ratio will persistently rise with the persistence of deficits $\overline{\text{def}}$ and low inflation. According to the Ricardian thesis, such a state does not persist. The temporal distribution of taxes implies that a stream of positive deficits over the nearer future will definitely be offset by higher taxes and negative deficits in the wider future. We should clearly recognize here the structure of the argument. A predetermined path of deficits $\overline{\text{def}}$ excluding "inflation taxes" proceeds in a "Ricardian World." The infinite intertemporal budget constraint thus imposes eventually an increase in taxes. But the predetermined characters of $\overline{\text{def}}$ and, implicitly, of ordinary taxes means that the inflation tax remains as the only possible adjustment to satisfy the infinite budget constraint. It thus follows that a noninflationary policy cannot be maintained over time in the context of a permanent deficit that is sufficiently large.

The infinite budget constraint reveals the nature of the problem. The single-period constraint

$$G_t + S_{t-1}(1 + i_{t-1}) = T_t + S_t + B_t - B_{t-1} \tag{29}$$

can be assembled into an intertemporal expression in terms of real magnitudes per unit of real income

$$\sum_{t=0}^{\infty} \left[\frac{1+n}{1+rr} \right]^t (g_t - t_t) + s_0 \frac{1+rr}{1+n} = \sum \left[\frac{1+n}{1+rr} \right]^t \frac{\Delta B_t}{B_t} \frac{1}{V}, \tag{30}$$

where V is the velocity of the monetary base. Once the left side is fixed at a substantial positive level, it follows that a very low growth of $\Delta B/B = \pi$ over an initial segment must be followed by larger monetary growth in the future.

The argument presented by Sargent and Wallace can be reconstructed along the following lines, using expression (30) above. The stock of real debt per unit of real income at time N satisfies

$$s(N) = s_0 + [\overline{\text{def}} - (\pi + n)b] \frac{\exp(rr - n)N}{rr - n}. \tag{31}$$

Under the assumption that $\overline{\text{def}} > (\pi + n)b$, the stock s grows monotonically with time N. Sargent and Wallace simply state that there exists ultimately a limit for s (somehow). The higher the levels reached by $s(N)$ the greater must be the subsequent inflation. This follows again from expression (29). Once an upper limit $\bar{s}$ is imposed with an unchanged $\overline{\text{def}}$, the inflation rate must adjust in accordance with

$$\bar{\pi} = \frac{\overline{\text{def}}}{b} + (rr - n)\frac{\bar{s}}{b} - n \ . \tag{32}$$

The positive relation between $\bar{\pi}$ and $\bar{s}$ is immediately obvious. A persistent accumulation of the real debt burden can ultimately always be terminated by sufficiently high levels of inflation.

Expression (32) can be used with two different interpretations according to the nature of the inequality between rr and n. With $rr > n$ it describes the inflation rate required to satisfy an imposed stock of relative real debt s. Alternatively, with $rr < n$ it determines the equilibrium stock s associated with any predetermined inflation rate; that is

$$s = \frac{\overline{\text{def}} - (\pi + n)b}{n - rr}. \tag{33}$$

In the first case fiscal and debt conditions dominate monetary policy, and in the second case monetary policy dominates the debt position.

The difference between the two states involving the nature of the adjustment to a constant real debt ratio s can be outlined in terms of Figure 3.4.

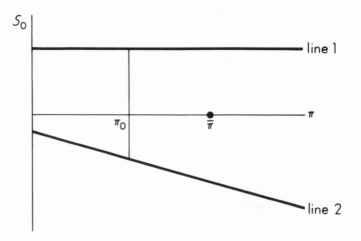

Figure 3.4

Line 1 represents the component $\overline{\text{def}} + (rr - n)s$ of $\overset{o}{s}$, and line 2 the component $[-(\pi + n)]b$. Now consider the first state with $rr > n$ and an inflation rate π_0 below the inflation rate $\bar{\pi}$ required to hold s constant. This means that the vertical distance between line 1 and the π-axis exceeds the vertical distance between the π-axis and line 2. The rate of change of s is positive under the circumstances, and line 1 drifts higher. This drift continues so long as the basic deficit $\overline{\text{def}}$ is maintained and π_0 is less than $\bar{\pi}$ [Eq. (32)]. In order to stablize the real debt ratio s, the inflation rate must be raised to the required rate $\bar{\pi}$, which rises with s. The higher line 1 was allowed to drift up, the further out to the right shifts $\bar{\pi}$.

In the second state characterized by $rr < n$, the real debt ratio s adjusts, in contrast, to any predetermined level π_0. Suppose the initial condition is again described by the graph. The real debt ratio s rises under the circumstances, and this *lowers* because $rr - n < 0$, line 1. This process persists until the vertical distance between line 1 and the π-axis coincides with the vertical distance between the π-axis and line 2.

Darby's (1984) rebuttal of the problem addressed by Sargent and Wallace concentrates essentially on the stability of the process and some observations supporting the required inequality. But the stability hardly removes the central issue brought to our attention by Sargent and Wallace. The following table reveals the problem. We are shown the equilibrium real debt ratio associated with various basic deficit ratios under a stable process.

$\overline{\text{def}}$	s
.01	.40
.05	2.40
.1	4.90

$$\pi = 0, \quad b = .05, \quad rr = .02, \quad n = .04$$

The assumptions made with respect to π, b, rr, and n are listed below the table. A glance at the table indicates that deficits of the order experienced or still expected in the United States and Europe would eventually produce, even in the context of a stable process, a massive increase in the real debt ratio from the current U.S. level of about .35. We should be reminded that this massive relative expansion of the government debt would occur in the context of a "non-Ricardian" world defined by $rr < n$.

Important real consequences emerge under the circumstances. Real rates of interest rise, and output is shifted from investment to consumption. Normal growth will consequently decline. The negative difference $rr - n$ may thus disappear, and the economy may move into an unstable debt accumulation process. The smaller (absolutely) the initial negative difference $rr - n$ and the larger the permanent deficit with the implicit equilibrium real debt ratio, the greater is the likelihood of a change in the sign of the crucial inequality.

The shift from $rr - n < 0$ to $rr - n > 0$ does not mean that the system necessarily assumes a "Ricardian property." The change in inequality is certainly consistent with such a property. It need not occur, however, because the inequality forms just a *necessary* condition for the Ricardian equivalence to occur. Persistence of a "non-Ricardian" world under the condition $rr > n$ aggravates, of course, the real consequences outlined above. These consequences especially induce the persistent rise of interest rates and the real debt burden. They eventually determine responses in the political arena that initiate an inflationary regime.

We should note that this argument is consistent with the monetarist and Keynesian analysis of the financial consequences associated with a budget deficit discussed in Section 2.3. The "monetarist" framework used 12 years ago for this purpose can easily be applied to the current problem. This common argument contrasts, however, with the argument attributed above to Sargent and Wallace in order to obtain the same result. The infinite budget constraint is made to impose the *eventual* inflationary solution. The Sargent–Wallace analysis suffers, however, from a troublesome indefiniteness associated with the arguments centered on infinite intertemporal budget constraints. The latter only conveys to agents that taxes must be adjusted *some time at an indeterminate* future in order to obey the constraint. The economic or social mechanism eventually producing the shift from debt finance to inflationary remains, moreover, quite obscure. A "Ricardian world" does not seem to provide such a mechanism. Sargent and Wallace suggest in passing the operation of limits of demand for securities. But such "limits" would be reflected in rising real interest rates and thus violate the "Ricardian pattern." The implicit indefiniteness in the world described by Sargent and Wallace means that agents are confronted with a substantial uncertainty with respect to timing, magnitude, and variance of the inflation tax.

This uncertainty is not recognized by the "Ricardian model." The resulting purchasing power risk associated with nominal bonds produces a risk premium represented by a covariance term (Baghat and Wakeman 1983) in the standard capital-asset pricing model. This risk premium is added to the basic (risk-free) real rate of interest to form the effective real rate. Considerations of uncertainty operating in the context of an infinite intertemporal budget constraint thus move the analysis beyond a "Ricardian world." The uncertain temporal reallocation of taxes produces real consequences affecting agents' real opportunities.

A cautionary note must be added. Once we abandon "nonlumping" taxes, the relevant real rate rr should be net of taxes on interest payments or receipts. Second, the relation between rr and n needs to be more carefully rephrased in order to avoid a relation between a risky return expressed by *n*—most especially once we acknowledge the relevance of a stochastic trend (Nelson and Plosser 1982; Stulz and Wasserfallen 1985), and a possibly riskless return to represent *rr*.

It was argued above that the stability of the debt process—that is, the sign of the difference $rr - n$—does not address our crucial problem raised by Sargent and Wallace. The crucial problem is the long-run danger of permanent inflation at a potentially massive scale.

The next table covering both states summarizes the long-run inflation threat associated with persistent deficits. The inflation rate is computed under the condition that the real debt

$$s = .33, b = .05 \text{ and } S = .5$$

$.06 = rr > n = .03$		$.02 = rr < n = .03$	
def	π	*def*	π
.01	39%	.01	10%
.05	139%	.05	90%
.10	239%	.10	190%

$.06 = rr > n = .03$		$.02 = rr < n = .03$	
def	π	*def*	π
.01	50%	.01	7%
.05	150%	.05	87%
.10	250%	.10	187%

ratio is held constant either at .33 or .5. We notice that, irrespective of the stability conditions $rr - n$, the long-run inflation threat embedded in a permanent basic deficit of 5 percent of gross national product would move us to levels not yet experienced as a maintained phenomenon in the United States or Europe.

4.2. The endogenous state of the monetary regime: a choice-theoretic analysis

The absence of any motivating force in the account presented by Sargent and Wallace explaining the eventual change in monetary regime directs our attention to McCallum's (1984) paper. The author adapts the model introduced by Sidrauski for his purpose. A representative agent maximizes the present value of current and future (instantaneous) utility over an infinite horizon. Instantaneous utility depends on real consumption and real money balances. Bonds, issued by the government, convey no direct utility to the agent. They do occur, however, in the agents' budget constraint. The agent is, moreover, visualized as a joint consuming-producing unit. A simple production technology is thus incorporated in the budget constraint. Maximization proceeds subject to the (infinite) set of these constraints. The first-order conditions yield restrictions on consumption c, real balances m, the stock of real capital k, the Lagrangian variable, and the usual inequality constraint bearing on the real rate of interest and the agent's bond holdings b. These conditions are supplemented with the government sector's budget constraint, which provides for finance of the deficit by means of money creation and bond issues. Consolidation of household and government constraint yields an income–expenditure statement in real terms.

A steady-state solution for all the relevant variables is easily satisfied under mixed bond–money financing. The steady-state condition requires that both money and bonds rise by equal percentages in this case. The deficit is, moreover, defined in the sense of the basic deficit exclusive of interest payments. Once the real deficit is fixed the associated percentage rise in nominal money balances determines the inflation rate. The optimality condition for real capital k yields the optimal stock by equating its marginal product with the exogenous utility rate of time preference. Insertion of the latter result into the consolidated constraint yields the optimal rate of consumption. The remaining first-order conditions determine real balances, Lagrangian multiplier and equality between the real rate of interest and the utility rate of time preference. The latter follows from the occurrence of a positive bond stock. Lastly, the magnitude of this stock is settled by the real version of the government's budget constraint.

The solution of the mixed finance carries through without a hitch and also satisfies the transversatility conditions. Similarly, financing the deficit with money only poses no problem. The argument proceeds as above. This case implies, however, that the real rate of interest remains below the utility rate of time preference. A problem arises, however, when the deficit, as defined, is only financed by bond issues. The transversatile conditions are violated in this case. There thus exists no steady-state solution for bond-financed permanent deficit. We also note that the real version of the government budget constraint would imply a *negative* steady-state stock of bonds that cannot be reconciled with the model.

McCallum demonstrates that the problem is quite sensitive to the specification of the deficit to be held constant. The pattern changes once we move beyond the basic deficit and includes the interest service on the outstanding debt. The transversatility condition is not violated for the stock of bonds once this extended deficit measure is held constant. This reflects the fact that the growth of real debt per capita does not explode as in the case of a constant "basic deficit" but actually converges to zero. The difference in this case is that the persistent increase in interest payments due to the rise in the stock of bonds is matched by corresponding increases in taxes. Last, McCallum establishes that a *permanently noninflationary bond-financed deficit can occur, provided* the growth rate of bonds is less than the utility rate of time preference. This implies that the basic deficit is negative and converges with time toward zero. The extended deficit remains, however, positive and converges to equality with the government's interest payments.

McCallum's analysis qualifies somewhat the central proposition advanced by Sargent and Wallace. A permanent deficit need not be inflationary and need not impose a change in the monetary regime. It depends partly on the nature of the policy rule specifying the permanent deficit. But McCallum's analysis still leaves unanswered a central issue in the Sargent–Wallace argument. We learn that a noninflationary bond-financed basic deficit is impossible. It is impossible because the steady-state system cannot produce that result. This answer does not attend to the question of why, in reality, initial attempts at a noninflationary finance of a basic deficit are eventually doomed. A similar problem involves the other result, suspending the Sargent–Wallace proposition. The analysis describes a world of certainty, perfect foresight, and nondistortionary taxes. The real variables are not affected by noninflationary finance under the circumstances. It was argued in an earlier section that the prevalence of distortionary taxes with uncertainty about the incidence of future taxes very likely modifies substantially this picture of a bond-financed permanent deficit. This case is reenforced by the remaining possibility that we live in a "non-Ricardian" world.

4.3. The empirical relevance of the issue

We still need to consider the relevance of the potential threat posed by a permanent large deficit to an anti-inflationary regime. The analysis offers by itself no evidence that an anti-inflationary policy executed in the present against a background of a permanent deficit policy cannot be maintained over the long run. A number of papers over the past years examined this issue. They investigated, in particular, whether persistent deficits eventually induced inflationary policies. Robert King and Charles Plosser (1985) offer for our purposes an excellent example of this literature. They first introduce some historical background and discuss the behavior characteristics of six different seignorage measures for the United States. They find that seignorage averaged over the period considered about three-tenths of 1 percent of gross national product. The various seignorage measures are also correlated for descriptive purposes with a range of important macro variables. The authors note here a correlation of .44 between the deficit and inflation over the postwar period.

> However, it is worthwhile to note that the correlation is essentially zero (.02) for the 1929–1952 period. By way of contrast, there appears to be a positive correlation between money creation and both real and nominal deficits in the 1929–1952 period.

There is, in general, no evidence for a contemporaneous relation between deficit and money creation in the United States. The underlying analysis does not stress, however, any particular contemporaneous relation but essentially an *intertemporal dynamic relation.* "The empirical strategy, therefore, is to look for a dynamic relation between revenue from money creation and deficits." The crucial question is whether past deficits explain subsequent revenues from money creation. The statistical results show "that seignorage does not appear to make a significant contribution to predicting any of the other government policy variables." Even more noteworthy is that deficits do not help predict seignorage.

The study extends attention beyond the United States. Among the eight nations outside Latin America only Italy exhibits some significant contemporaneous correlation between national income account deficits and money creation. The four Latin American nations included show, in contrast, some significant contemporaneous correlation between these magnitudes. An investigation of *dynamic intertemporal* interrelation confirms, however, the results obtained for the United States. Switzerland forms an exception. This is somewhat surprising and makes, against the background of Swiss financial institutions, little systematic sense.

The study demonstrates that we so far possess little systematic evidence about the dynamic link between current fiscal policy and future monetary policy. The problem may have barely confronted Western nations over most of the postwar period. But the experience of Italy, Israel (Fischer 1984), and Argentina (Dutton 1971), and more casual observations from other nations does suggest that we should not rely on the persistence of the monetary regime observed over the sample period in a radically different fiscal context. The dynamic link emphasized by Sargent and Wallace hardly emerges in contexts of the modest deficits dominantly prevailing in the United States and some other nations until recently. The issue has thus just been opened, and King and Plosser offer a useful starting point for future explorations of the subject. But such explorations need to attend to a subtle but basic analytic issue. We encounter here a generalization of the problem faced in the old fiscalist debate. It is anything but clear how the relevant fiscal variables need be specified. In particular, it is not obvious that the official administrative deficit, the national income account deficit, or some real versions of these measures form the relevant magnitude for the analysis of our problem. Kotlikoff (1984) raised some searching questions about the standard measures of deficits. These questions extend to the analysis of any possible relation between budgetary operations and subsequent monetary regimes.

4.4. The deficit and economic activity

Traditional Keynesian and neo-Keynesian analysis suffered no doubt that lower income taxes or higher government expenditures raise economic activity. The presumed permanent inefficiency of the economy could be expected to offer a leverage for fiscal policy to influence output and employment. Recent experience with large deficits expected to persist into an indefinite future generated in the public arena increasing doubts about their beneficial effects. Analysis based on "non-Ricardian" assumptions emphasized, of course, for a long time the negative long-term effect of permanent deficits. These effects operate via the asset market on capital accumulation and normal output. Public doubts concentrate, however, for a variety of reasons on the short run effects associated with deficits. Voices emerged that argued that deficits actually exert a contractionary effect and lower output in the short run independent of further effects on normal output growth. Academia could hardly stay behind the new developments. The issue certainly deserves examination. Two papers are selected in order to probe the argument of "contractionary deficits" or "perverse fiscal policy."

Feldstein (1984a) recently explored the possibility of a "contractionary deficit." His analysis revives an argument widely used by Keynesians in the 1950s to explain in real terms a persistent inflationary drift. Prices are supposed to be asymmetrically responsive to positive and negative changes in demand. Allocative demand shocks are converted under the circumstances into a persistent inflationary drift. Sectors experiencing rising real demands raise prices by a substantial margin, whereas sectors exposed to shrinking real demand lower their price, at most, quite modestly. This idea is exploited by placing fiscal policy within an environment of specific interacting sectors. Feldstein initially presents a simple argument along the following line. Suppose income taxes are reduced. Consumption demand rises and investment falls. The latter follows from higher interest rates. Consumption goods prices rise, whereas investment goods prices remain unchanged. The increase in the price level against a constant velocity and money stock necessarily lowers the level of output. Lower taxes thus lower output.

This suggestive argument motivates a more general and explicit analysis based on the following summary structure:

$$X = C_h + C_g + I_h + I_g, \tag{34}$$

$$\Pi_c(C) \cdot C + \Pi_I(I) \cdot I = v(r + \pi) \cdot M, \tag{35}$$

$$C = C_h + C_g, \qquad I = I_h + I_g, \tag{36}$$

where X = real income, C = real total consumption composed of house-hold consumption C_h and government consumption C_g, I = real total investment consisting of household investment I_h and government invest-ment I_g, r = real rate of interest, Π = expected rate of inflation, M = money stock, $\Pi_c(C)$ = price level of consumption goods as a function of C, $\Pi_I(I)$ = price level of investment goods as a function of I, and v = monetary velocity.

All variables in Eq. (34) occur in real terms. The simple addition of the components C and I in order to sum up to real income will not hold, in general, for a multisector specification with variable relative prices. Feld-stein therefore postulates units for C and I that uniformly assure unit prices in the initial position.

Expression (35) states a quantity equation. The left side represents nominal income and the right side nominal demand. The structure is completed by introducing a consumption function and an investment function:

$$C_h = \phi(X - T), \qquad I_h = \psi(r). \tag{37}$$

T refers to income taxes.

Expressions (34), (35), and (37) can be represented in a simple diagram. Line 1 in Figure 3.5. describes Eq. (34), and line 2 Eq. (35). The signs of the slopes are immediately established by inspection, and so are the direc-tions of the shift induced by a reduction in taxes T. Both lines are shifted up, increasing the real rate of interest. The effect on real income remains ambiguous without additional constraints. Feldstein specifies three conditions sufficient to produce a shift of the intersection point to the northwest, as indicated in the graph. These conditions are (i) a low-interest elasticity of monetary velocity, (ii) a large-interest elasticity of investment, (iii) a high elasticity of Π with respect to C.

The formal exercise certainly produces the desired perverse fiscal policy. Its relevance remains, however, quite doubtful. The analysis appears strangely regressive at this time. Important price-theoretical contributions are disregarded, and we revert to a peculiarly ancient Keynesian world. Analytically more serious is a basic logical flaw. Movements along line 1 and of shifts in its position hold prices constant at unity by construction. Movements along line 2 and shifts in its position modify prices Π_C and Π_I. Any shift of line L along 2 thus modifies prices under the assump-

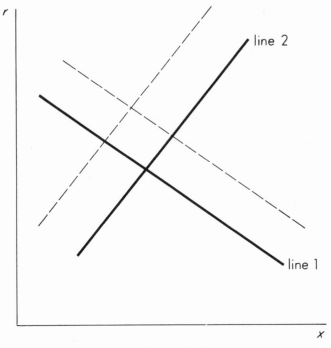

Figure 3.5

tions of unchanged prices. The same contradiction appears whenever line 2 is shifted along line 1. A change in T (or C_g, I_g) is thus analyzed within a framework exhibiting a flawed structure. This contradiction would seem to remove all significance from this attempt to establish a presumption for a "contractionary deficit."

Consider now an alternative procedure to move into a new world of fiscal policy analysis that reverses a long-accepted result of Keynesian analysis. Mankiw and Summers (1984) explored this possibility in the context of a slightly modified, but otherwise thoroughly standard, IS/LM analysis.

$$Y = C(Y - T, r) + I(Y, r) + G, \tag{38}$$

$$M = L(C, I, G, r). \tag{39}$$

The letters designating the relevant magnitudes assume their usual meaning. The modification applies to the money demand in Eq. (39). Money demand depends separately on the three expenditure components. Mankiw and Summers essentially concentrate on consumption C as the relevant scale variable. The multiplier of income Y with respect to T is immediately determined as

$$\frac{\partial Y}{\partial T} = \frac{C_Y[(L_C - L_I)I_r - L_r]}{\Delta},\tag{40}$$

where $\Delta = -[1 - C_Y - I_Y]\cdot[L_I\cdot I_r + L_C\cdot C_r + L_r]$

$$- [I_r + C_r]\cdot[L_C\cdot C_Y + L_I\cdot I_Y] > 0.$$

The detailed structure of the positive denominator Δ need not concern us here. It follows that the standard result holds according to the necessary and sufficient condition

$$\frac{\partial Y}{\partial T} < 0 \quad \text{iff} \quad L_C < L_I + \frac{L_r}{I_r}.\tag{41}$$

A necessary and sufficient condition for a "perverse response" can now be given as

$$\frac{\partial Y}{\partial T} > 0 \quad \text{iff} \quad \epsilon(L, C) > \left[\epsilon(L, I) + \frac{\epsilon(L, r)}{\epsilon(I, r)}\right] \frac{C}{I},$$

where $\epsilon(y, x)$ denotes the elasticity of y with respect to x. The major portion of the paper offers a valiant attempt to present a case for the crucial inequality yielding a positive tax multiplier. The discussion assumes that $L_I = L_g = 0$.

The authors first assess with some rough calculations the crucial inequality. They assemble for this purpose available estimates and income account data. The results confirm the condition. Similar calculations suggest, moreover, that the expenditure multiplier is little affected by the change in specification. With a value less than one it is hardly a "multiplier," however. The tax multiplier, in contrast, changes sign.

A survey of the literature indicates to the author the superiority of permanent income or wealth as a scale variable. The permanent-income hypothesis of consumption suggests, under the circumstances, that consumption would offer a good proxy for the scale variable. The choice of consumption is further supported in the eyes of the authors by the ownership distribution of money. Measures comparing the variability of velocity derived from a variety of scale variables, and the results obtained from money demand regressions appear to offer more significant evidence in this context. The first difference of a consumption velocity based on $M1$ exhibits the lowest variability. Similarly, the regressions assign, in general, a dominant weight to consumption compared to national income, disposable income and final sales, or total private spending as a scale variable.

The reservations about the traditional Keynesian tax policy are developed on the basis of a framework very close to those underlying the original fiscalist debate and judged to be unsatisfactory at the time by some Keynesian participants. Mankiw and Summers nevertheless raised a relevant point that may be robust beyond the simple IS/LM formulation used. An examination of the Brunner–Meltzer (1976) model reveal that the impact of a tax cut on income from human wealth is substantially attenuated by wealth and substitution effects on asset markets. A tax cut on income from nonhuman wealth produces a stronger response. The two tax cuts induce, moreover, opposite shifts between consumption and investment. These distinctions are glossed over by Mankiw and Summers and so are the substitution responses conditioned by distortionary taxes. Their explorations could be interpreted to mean that the short-run stabilization function of tax policies should be recognized as a questionable exercise. Comparatively much more important are long-run aspects of tax policies shaping the use and development of an economy's resources.

4.5. The behavior of deficits

With the beginning of this decade, fiscal policy and deficits became a major theme attracting public attention. Wall Street and the media assigned increasing importance to the deficit. There emerged a widening conviction that we entered a new era characterized by large permanent deficits. This conviction essentially suggests that the nature of the process determining the behavior of deficits in the United States substantially changed by the end of the 1970s. Such a change would reflect the emergence of a new pattern in the political process controlling the deficit. The occurrence of a structural break in policy regime cannot be excluded a priori. But our impressions of the past four years offer no relevant evidence in support of the thesis. In order to judge our situation we need a theory about the process controlling the deficit. Guided by such a theory, suitable tests yield some evidence on the thesis asserting the recent emergence of a new fiscal regime in the United States.

For most of the postwar period there was little reason to address this issue. Macro analysis thus neglected to develop a theory about the behavior of deficits. Barro's (1981a,b; 1984a,b) prolific contributions attend in recent years also to this dimension of fiscal policy. The basic idea guiding the research emphasizes that tax rates are essentially adjusted to perceived permanent government expenditures. Their response to perceived temporary changes in government expenditures remains, under the circumstances, quite modest. Tax revenues thus behave much more smoothly over time than actual government expenditures. A first study by Barro derives the tax-smoothing behavior from the government's optimizing behavior addressed to the minimization of the excess burden imposed by taxes on the economy. Bond-financed deficits associated with temporary bulges in government expenditures are thus designed to minimize the social cost of taxation. The specific simple theory elaborated in Barro's first study (1981a) actually implies that optimal tax policy sets a constant tax rate over time. This view was recently contested by Feldstein (1984b). This argument emphasizes that we need to compare the social cost of changes in tax rates adjusted to finance transitory bulges in government expenditures with the social costs of smaller but permanent tax rate increases needed to finance the additional interest payments resulting from the prior bond financing. An incorporation of plausible parameter values into this analysis suggests that tax financing of temporary government expenditures is superior to debt financing, provided the economy's stock of real capital is smaller than its optimal magnitude. Feldstein emphasizes, moreover, that in the case of permanent expenditure there exists essentially no financial choice. One way or the other these expenditures are covered by taxes. This analysis seems to imply that the optimal stock of public debt is zero.

Feldstein's analysis obviously cannot provide the starting point for an empirical analysis of deficits and public debt even if we accept its relevance as a benchmark for a welfare analysis of budgetary operations. Any positive interpretation of the essentially normative analysis is, moreover, immediately disconfirmed by the facts. Lastly, an evaluation of the normative analysis as a benchmark for welfare statements lies beyond the range addressed in this paper. But its normative relevance does not preclude that intertemporal tax smoothing may offer a good basis for an analysis of deficit behavior. This smoothing pattern may be explained very differently from Barro's initial formulation that was questioned by Feldstein. It thus seems quite appropriate that Barro simply postulates a tax-smoothing pattern in his most recent examination. This hypothesis is actually formulated in its most rigid form as a constant tax rate. The basic idea is, however, consistent with some contingent flexibility of tax rates over time.

The hypothesis to be tested is constituted by two building blocks. The first introduces the tax-smoothing hypothesis, and the second combines it with the specification of deficit in terms of the budget constraint. The tax-smoothing hypothesis is applied to an intertemporal budget constraint in order to determine the expected constant tax rate. This constraint is

$$\int_0^\infty g(t)e^{-rt}\,dt\,+\,b(0)\,=\,\int_0^\infty \tau(t)y(t)e^{-rt}\,dt, \tag{42}$$

where $g(t)$ designates real government expenditures, b the inherited stock of real debt, τ the tax rate, and $y(t)$ the portion of income forming the tax base. Equation (42) immediately implies the condition for a constant tax rate:

$$\tau = \frac{\int_0^\infty g(t)e^{-rt}\,dt + b(0)}{\int_0^\infty y(t)e^{-rt}\,dt}. \tag{43}$$

This condition can be transformed to yield a statement relating the tax rate with permanent government expenditures g^* and permanent income Y^*. These permanent levels perceived at the intitial time $t = 0$ involve two assumptions. The first specifies a trend growth rate n for g and y such that the present value of g (or y) along the trend equals the present value of the actual future course of g (or y). We thus obtain

$$\int_0^\infty g(0) \cdot e^{-(r-n)t}\,dt = \int_0^\infty g(t)e^{-rt}\,dt \tag{44}$$

and a similar expression for y. Secondly, the permanent levels g^* (and y^*) are then defined by the condition

$$g^*(0) = (r - n)\int_0^\infty g(t)e^{-rt}\,dt, \tag{45}$$

$$y^*(0) = (r - n)\int_0^\infty y(t)e^{-rt}\,dt.$$

This condition establishes a relation between the present value of $g(t)$ (or $y(t)$) and its permanent level of g. A suitable replacement in expression (42) yields the desired relation between the average tax rate τ and the permanent magnitudes

$$\tau = \frac{g^* + (r - n)b(0)}{y^*}. \tag{46}$$

The second building block invokes the budget constraint expressed in real terms

$$\frac{db}{dt} = g + rb - \tau y, \tag{47}$$

where b represents the stock of real debt. Replacing τ in (47) with the aid of (46) and rearranging terms yields the basic relation

$$\frac{db}{dt} = \left[1 - \frac{y}{y^*}\right][g^* + (r - n)b] + (g - g^*) + nb. \tag{48}$$

The first term describes a cyclical effect. The deficit increases during recession and recedes during upswings. The effect of the business cycle on the deficit increases, moreover, with g^*. The second term—that is, $(r - n)b$—within the bracket is negligible and can be disregarded. The second term indicates that temporary government expenditures affect the deficit one for one. Lastly, the third term reflects the financing of interest payments on outstanding debt made possible by the "normal growth" in debt corresponding to the trend growth of the economy. This item unavoidably occurs once we assume a constant tax rate. Otherwise the relative interest burden would fall and tax rates could not be constant.

Equation (48) describes the growth of real debt as of any path of the price level. It follows that multiplying both sides of Eq. (48) with the price variable does not adequately render the growth of nominally valued debt B. The expression πB multiplying the inflation rate with the stock B must be added. We thus obtain

$$\frac{dB}{dt} = (n + \pi)B + \left[1 - \frac{y}{y^*} \right] Pg^* + P(g - g^*). \qquad (49)$$

One more term must be added, however. The structure of this last term depends on whether the debt variable is measured at market or at par value. In either case the dependent variable is modified over time whenever the average market rate of interest changes.

The underlying analysis ultimately yields the following regression:

$$\frac{B_t - B_{t-1}}{P_t Y_c} = a_0 \frac{B_{t-1}}{P_{t-1}Y_{t-1}} + a_1 \pi_t \frac{B_{t-1}}{P_{t-1}Y_{t-1}} \qquad (50)$$

$$+ a_2 \text{YVAR} + a_3 \text{GVAR} + a_4 \text{RVAR} + U_c.$$

YVAR refers either to $(1 - y/y^*) (g^*/y_t)$ or to an expression based on the unemployment rate related to the first by a modified "Okun's law." Either formulation reflects the cyclic influence on the deficit. GVAR expresses the temporary government expenditures, and RVAR the adjustment required to reflect the effect of changes in interest rates on market or par value of debt B. The hypothesis summarized by Eq. (50) implies that

$$a_0 = n \quad \text{and} \quad a_1 = a_2 = a_3 = 1. \qquad (51)$$

An extensive range of empirical examinations substantially confirms the component $a_1 = 1$ of the total hypothesis. The confirmation holds for the whole sample 1920–82, for the sample without the war, and subsamples 1920–40 or 1950–82. The coefficient a_3 on temporary government expenditures lies between .5 and .6 for the whole sample and drops to .22 whenever the war data are deleted. The results from the subsamples confirm this pattern. The largest estimate is .16. Two estimates out of 12 are (nonsignificantly) negative, and ten are smaller than their respective standard error. We observe here no confirmation of the hypothesis. All estimates of a_3 are very significantly below unity. The "cyclic coefficient" a_2, in contrast, is uniformly positive and highly significant for all estimation periods and choices of YVAR. The coefficient estimate, however, occurs systematically on the high side. It clusters around 1.5. This result is not consistent with the strict tax smoothing hypothesis. It reveals a measure of cyclical flexibility in tax rates. Lastly, the estimate of a_0 appears to be persistently too low as an estimate of the trend growth in real GNP.

The regression analysis so far yields no evidence that the current decade ushered in a new regime of budgetary processes. The observations on the deficit cast up by the four years 1980–83 are quite compatible with the patterns observed in past years. The estimated deficit traces the actual value quite well, and the residuals remain in the usual range. The regression even overpredicts the deficit for three out of four years. Barro's results also imply that realization of the CBO's baseline projections over the next five years would indicate a break in the structure of the process generating deficits. We would then actually have moved into a new policy regime. An unchanged policy regime would require substantial adjustments in expenditures and tax revenues in order to stay below the CBO projections.

The estimates of the coefficients associated with temporary government expenditures confront us with a serious and frequently occurring problem associated with the evaluation of hypotheses. Approximation errors in the measurement of specific variables may burden the statistical work with an uncertain interpretation. It is, in the present context, quite likely that the measurement of temporary government expenditures contains a substantial and variable error margin. But we know, of course, that measurement errors in the regressor bias the coefficient estimates toward zero. This problem is worsened by the fact that the sample period 1920–82 contains a single major observation for temporary government expenditures offered by World War II. Small values and little variation in this variable over most of the sample period combined with a potentially significant measurement error obscure the message of the data. A discriminating evaluation is not possible under the circumstances. It is very difficult to decide whether the results bearing on a_3 summarized above should be interpreted as a rejection of the hypothesis ($a_3 = 1$) or can be reconciled with the hypothesis on the basis of the data problems indicated. A possible strategy to further explore the matter involves a search for data with more "action" and experimenting with different approaches to the measurement of theoretical entities as, for instance, in this case, the g^* variable. Barro (1985) examined these opportunities with another paper exploiting British data for the period 1730–1918. These data exhibit much more variation in temporary government expenditures produced by military spending. The statistical investigation deletes the cyclic component. No reliable data seem to be available for this magnitude. This omission may partly explain the serial correlations of the regression residual. The regression estimated was confined to the two terms

$$\frac{B_t - B_{t-1}}{P_t Y_t} = a_0 \frac{B_{t-1}}{P_{t-1} Y_{t-1}} + a_1 \hat{g}_t + w_t, \qquad (52)$$

where $\hat{g}_t$ denotes temporary government expenditures, and w a random term. The first term in this formulation summarizes the first two terms of Eq. (50). The hypothesis thus implies that a_0 is equal to the sum of trend growth n plus the average inflation rate over the sample period 1755–1918. The estimate $a_0 = .021$ coincides remarkably well with this sum. The estimate for a_1 moves, moreover, much closer to unity (i.e., $a_1 = .9$) than in the case of the United States. This estimate is two standard errors from unity. The British data thus confirm the essential idea of the underlying hypothesis, but they do suggest some contingent tax adjustments.

The analysis of deficit behavior introduced a new dimension into macroanalysis. The public discussion erupting in recent years speculating about structural changes in our fiscal processes reveals the relevance of this emerging research. Barro deserves some credit for raising the issue in advance of the public arena's attention. The exploration of the "Ricardian theme" eventually led to an examination of deficits and public debt. We are hardly in a position at this stage to accept Barro's hypothesis with any sense of conviction. The evidence is still too unclear in this respect. But neither can we reject it. So far, it is "the only game in town."

5. Concluding Remarks

The professional discussion of fiscal policy has moved a long way over the past 20 years. The "great debate of the 1960s" centered on the role of fiscal policy expressed by the effect of expenditures and taxes on national income and economic activity. This discussion did modify the earlier position of the postwar period represented by the works referred to in Section 2. There seemed also to ensue by the early 1970s a consensus that fiscal policy did probably produce permanent nominal effects and temporary real macro effects. There remained substantial controversy about magnitude and temporal patterns of the consequences. There also persisted a basic disagreement about the role of fiscal operations in a concept of stabilization policy. An activist exploitation of fiscal instruments for purposes of short-run stabilization was typically advocated by the Keynesians. This contrasts with a more classical conception advocated by scholars with a monetarist and neoclassical view. This view rejects short-run manipulations and advocates policies addressed to the establishment of an institutional framework, not to sequences of fiscal actions. Such an "institutional policy" should provide an essentially confined, and thus reliably predictable, pattern of fiscal operations. This issue will be considered in the last paragraphs.

The temptation to sneer at the empirical work executed at the time seems, on occasion, irresistible. It would indeed be pointless to reproduce such investigations today. It would also express some measure of incompetence relative to the state of current economic and statistical analysis. But this work had a function at the time and was not irrelevant with respect to a strong thrust embedded in the Keynesian message. It did contribute to modifying positions even when not explicitly acknowledged. Modigliani's presidential address to the American Economic Association (1977) had a different flavor than the Keynesian stories of the 1950s. We note on the other side at least some monetarists with a more explicit recognition of fiscal variables than before. An unpalatable fact found, however, little resonance at the time. The central (non-price-theoretic) emphasis assigned in Keynesian analysis to income–expenditure flows made it quite sensitive to the choice of "autonomous expenditures." This choice seems anything but settled. The meaning of traditional Keynesian theory, on an empirical level beyond formal classroom exercises, remains obscure.

More recent discussions of fiscal impact on the macro behavior of the economy may usefully lead us beyond this impasse. The market or coordination failure conception underlying the Keynesian approach naturally produced an analysis downplaying the role of prices with an emphasis on interacting income–expenditure flows. The classic tradition rejects the basic failure conception motivating Keynesian analysis. A framework emphasizing a system of ("multiplying") interacting flows is thus replaced with an essentially price-theoretical conception. This conception should not be identified, however, with a (total) market-clearing analysis. The price-theoretical approach developed by Barro includes, moreover, the important distinction between anticipated and unanticipated fiscal events or, most particularly, recognizes the differential impact of temporary and permanent fiscal actions. The multiplier effect essentially vanishes in this price-theoretical context. The consequences of fiscal events, moreover, depend crucially on the government sector's use of the goods and services acquired from the private sector. Once we abandon the sinkhole theory, new channels of influence are recognized. Barro's analysis shows, for instance, that the impact of government expenditures on goods and services depends significantly on their "supply-side effects." This differs radically from the "demand-side dominance" of Keynesian analysis. This analytic evolution, initially suggested by Martin Bailey, still needs further elaboration. The operation of the government sector involves more than a pure redirection of privately produced goods within the private sector. It should be recognized as a production sector absorbing inputs converted into an output. The difference in the incentive structure between private and public sectors implies an important difference between the production functions of the two sectors. We also need to consider to which extent these consequences associated with the government sector as a production sector bear more significantly on longer-term aspects of an economy.

The dimensions covered by fiscal policy were significantly extended with the introduction of the Ricardian theme. The "Ricardian equivalence theorem" defines a useful benchmark for our professional discussions. It obliges the advocates of a more or less "conventional thesis" to specify the conditions responsible for the real consequences of the government's decisions how to finance expenditures. The possible recognition of a pure debt effect on real variables, explicitly acknowledged by the "stability analysis" of the early 1970s, would hardly suffice today. The discussion unleashed over the years directed our attention to new mechanisms or channels of influence conveying real impulses from the government's financial decisions. The association of deficit finance with intergenerational transfers, the role of uncertainty and risk related with future tax liabilities, and the condition of intergenerational transfers linked with the function of bequests deserve critical exploration by the profession. We may yet convince ourselves that the government's "financial mix" does exert some real consequences but, to some extent, for reasons beyond the pure debt effect. We also note that the extension of fiscal analysis summarized above increasingly directs our attention to a range of influences modifying the division of total output between real consumption, household real capital, and real capital used in the production process. These channels condition normal output. Their operation may be more important than the immediate impact on total output.

The emergence of an apparently persistent deficit was bound to attract the profession's interest. Attempts to justify some public concern that "deficits are contractionary" are so far at best speculatively "interesting." More significant seems to be the attempt to explain the observable behavior of deficits. A useful explanation would offer a criterion for judging the occurrence of changes in fiscal regime. The issue raised by Sargent and Wallace also deserves serious further attention. It involves a basic question about the political role of monetary and fiscal institutions and the relevant deficit measure guiding policy. The problem arises whenever fiscal institutions dominate the monetary institutions over the longer horizon. Political economy analysis seems to support this assumption. It follows under the circumstances that a breakdown of the "Victorian rule" (Buchanan 1985) ultimately determines an inflationary adjustment of monetary policy. The nature of the monetary regime ultimately depends on the prevailing fiscal regime. A noninflationary monetary regime thus requires for its survival a fiscal regime approximating a 'Victorian rule." But the analysis of this issue remained somewhat incomplete. The economic and political mechanism creating the accommodation of monetary policy to a permanent deficit still requires some attention. The empirical relevance is also unresolved at this time. There so far exists little supportive evidence, but then we may have only entered the age of permanent deficits.

Finally, a basic issue of political economy should be faced. The contrasting conceptions of fiscal policy offered by the Keynesian vision and the classical tradition were characterized in a previous paragraph. The issue cannot be left unattended with the easy escape into "ideology." There is more involved that deserves the careful attention of the political economist.

Three substantive issues condition the policy conception: the basic coordination failure of a market economy, the information problem confronting policymakers, and the characteristic operation of political institutions. Some Keynesians emphasize that the basic coordination failure of market economies necessitates the intervention of the government in order to offset this failure. Such intervention exploits to a large extent the powers of fiscal policy. The coordination failure to be corrected with the aid of fiscal policy involves, moreover, both a short-run and a long-run dimension. The latter dominated the attention at the end of World War II with the projections of oversaving and secular stagnation. This "structural coordination failure" justifies a permanent large deficit to offset private oversaving. This portion of the Keynesian argument offers no basis for *activist* manipulation of fiscal policy or for a large government sector. Activist manipulation follows from an emphasis of a "dynamic coordination failure" that produces inefficient fluctuations in output and employment.

One strand of the issue thus depends on the substantive question of a long-run (structural) coordination problem. The view advanced by Keynesians in this respect forty years ago was thoroughly disconfirmed by the end of the 1950s. The issue remains, however, as we still encounter assertions that an economy may be trapped within a set of multiple "underemployment equilibria." The other strand, represented by the "dynamic coordination failure," constituting the case for an activist fiscal policy, involves three distinct substantive issues. We note first the idea that fluctuations in output and employment are inherently inefficient. The reviving interest in "real business cycle theories" warns us, however, that economic fluctuations are not necessarily inefficient. The analysis developed by Stulz and Wasserfallen (1985) demonstrates, moreover, that economic fluctuations may reflect the characteristics of financial regimes. But this cautionary note is really just a special case of the general information problem faced by policymakers. The activist argument implicitly assumes that policymakers do possess reliable and detailed knowledge about the dynamic properties of the economy. Such knowledge would certainly allow the pursuit of an effective fiscal intervention. But such knowledge, while necessary, is not a sufficient condition for socially successful fiscal activism. We still need to invoke a goodwill or public-interest theory or benevolent dictator view of government. The case for fiscal activism, at least for purposes of stabilization policy, thus involves two important empirical assumptions bearing on required information and the behavior of man in political contexts. The case for an "institutional policy" rests, in contrast, on the empirical proposition that the two crucial conditions postulated by advocates of activism do not hold in reality. We lack the needed *detailed* and *reliable* knowledge about the economy's dynamic structure. The range of analytic results and empirical positions covered in the survey demonstrates this state most explicitly. The consequences of this information problem are reenforced by the fact that self-interested behavior also permeates the political environment. There is little evidence that political agencies operate according to a generally recognized social welfare function. Fiscal activism produces, under the circumstances, more problems. We have no assurance that it will not *generate* truly inefficient fluctuations. These issues associated with the political economy of fiscal policy are wide open and far from settled at this stage. We may yet achieve some cognitive progress in this field once we recognize the substantive nature of the problems behind the ideological smoke.

References

Ando, A. and F. Modigliani. 1965. The relative stability of monetary velocity and the investment multiplier. *American Economic Review* 55: 696–728.

———1976. Impacts of fiscal actions on aggregate income and the monetarist controversy: Theory and evidence. In *Monetarism*, ed. J.L. Stein. Amsterdam: North-Holland.

Andersen, L.C. and J.L. Jordan. 1968. Monetary and fiscal actions: A test of their relative importance in economic stabilization. *Federal Reserve Bank of St. Louis Review* 50: 11–24.

Aschauer, D. 1985. Fiscal Policy and Aggregate Demand. *American Economic Review* 75: 117–27.

Aschauer, D. and J. Greenwood. 1985. Macroeconomic effects of fiscal policy. In *Carnegie–Rochester Conference Series on Public Policy,* Vol. 23. Forthcoming.

Baghat, S. and L.M. Wakeman. 1983. Non-diversifiable inflation risk and expected treasury bill returns. Working paper, University of Rochester, Rochester, New York.

Bailey, M.J. 1971. *National Income and the Price Level.* New York: McGraw-Hill.

Baltensperger, Ernst. 1984. The public debt: Limits and effects. Working paper, University of Bern, Bern, Switzerland.

Barro, R.J. (1978). The impact of social security on private saving: Evidence from the U.S. time series. *American Enterprise Institute,* pp. 1–36.

_____ 1981a. *Money, Expectations, and Business Cycles: Essays in Macroeconomics.* New York: Academic Press.

_____ 1981b. Output effects of government purchases. *Journal of Political Economy* 89: 1086–1121.

_____ 1984a. *Macroeconomics.* New York: Wiley.

_____ 1984b. U.S. deficits since World War I. Working paper, University of Rochester, Rochester, New York.

_____ 1985. Government spending, interest rates, prices and budget deficits in the U.K. 1730–1918. Working Paper No. 1, Rochester Center for Economic Research, University of Rochester.

Barsky, R.B., N.G. Mankiw, and S.P. Zeldes. 1984. Ricardian consumers with Keynesian propensities. NBER Working Paper Series, No. 1400.

Bernheim, E.D., A. Schleifer, and L.H. Summers. 1985. Bequests as a means of payment. *Journal of Political Economy.* Forthcoming.

Blanchard, Olivier. 1984. Debt, deficits and finite horizons. NBER Working Paper Series.

Blinder, A.S. and R.M. Solow. 1974. *The Economics of Public Finance.* Washington, D.C.: Brookings Institute.

_____ 1976. Does fiscal policy still matter? A reply. *Journal of Monetary Economics* 2: 501–10.

Bomhoff, E.J. 1983. *Monetary Uncertainty.* Amsterdam: North-Holland.

Boskin, M.J. and L.J. Kotlikoff. 1985. Public debt and U.S. saving: A new test of the neutrality hypothesis. *Carnegie–Rochester Conference Series on Public Policy,* Vol. 23. Forthcoming.

Brunner, K. 1951. Inconsistency and indeterminacy in classical economics. *Econometrica,* 19: 152–73.

_____ 1970. Ein Neuformulierung der Quantitatstheorie des Geldes. *Kredit und Kapital.* 1–30.

_____ 1971. Survey of selected issues in monetary theory. *Schweitzerische Zeutschrift fur Volkswirtschaft und Statistik* 107 (1).

_____ 1976. Inflation, money and the role of fiscal arrangements: An analytical framework for the inflation problem. In *The New Inflation and Monetary Policy,* ed. M. Monti. New York: MacMillan.

Brunner, K. and A.H. Meltzer. 1972a. Money, debt and economic activity: An alternative approach. *Journal of Political Economy* 80: 951–77.

_____ 1972b. A monetarist framework for aggregate analysis. In *Proceedings of the First Konstanzer Seminar on Monetary Theory and Monetary Policy,* ed. K. Brunner. Berlin: Drunker and Humblot.

_____ 1976. An aggregative theory for a closed economy, and Reply. Monetarism: The principal issues: Areas of argument and the work remaining. In *Monetarism,* ed. J.L. Stein. Amsterdam: North-Holland.

Buchanan, J. 1985. Budgetary bias and post-Keynesian politics. In *Growth of Government*, eds. A. Lindbeck and J. Myrman.

Buiter, W. and J. Tobin. 1978. *Debt Neutrality: A Brief Review of Doctrine and Evidence*. Manuscript.

Carlson, K. 1967. The federal budget and economic stabilization. *Federal Reserve Bank of St. Louis Review* 49: 5–12.

Chan, L.K.C. 1983. Uncertainty and the neutrality of government financing decisions. *Journal of Monetary Economics* 11: 351–72.

Christ, C.F. 1968. A simple macroeconomic model with a budget constraint. *Journal of Political Economy* 76: 53–67.

_____ 1979. On fiscal and monetary policies and the government budget constraint. *American Economic Review* 69: 526–38.

Darby, M.R. 1984. Some pleasant monetarist arithmetic. *Federal Reserve Bank of Minneapolis Quarterly Review* 8: 15–20.

DeLeeuw, F. and J. Kalchbrenner. 1969. Monetary and fiscal actions: A test of their relative importance in economic stabilization—A comment. *Federal Reserve Bank of St. Louis Review* 51: 6–11.

DePrano, M. and T. Mayer. 1965. Tests of the relative importance of autonomous expenditures and money. *American Economic Review* 55: 729–52.

Dutton, D. S. 1971. A model of self-generating inflation: The Argentine case. *Journal of Money, Credit, and Banking* 3: 245–62.

Evans, P. 1984. The effects on output of money growth and interest rate volatility in the United States. *Journal of Political Economy* 92: 204–22.

Feldstein, M. 1978. The impact of social security on private saving: Evidence from the U.S. time series: A Reply. *American Enterprise Institute*, 37–47.

_____ 1982. Government deficits and aggregate demand. *Journal of Monetary Economics* 9: 1–20.

_____ 1984a. Can an increased budget deficit be contractionary? NBER Working Paper Series.

_____ 1984b. Debt and taxes in the theory of public finance. NBER Working Paper Series.

Fischer, S. 1984. The economy of Israel. In *Monetary and Fiscal Policies and Their Applications*. In *Carnegie–Rochester Conference Series on Public Policy*, Vol. 20, 7–52.

Fischer, S. and R.C. Merton. 1984. Macroeconomics and finance: The role of the stock market. In *Carnegie–Rochester Conference Series on Public Policy*, Vol. 21, 57–108.

Friedman, M. 1952. Price, income, and monetary changes in three wartime periods. *American Economic Review* 42: 612–25.

Friedman, M. and D. Meiselman. 1963. The relative stability of monetary velocity and the investment multiplier in the United States, 1897–1958. In *Stabilization Policies*. Englewood Cliffs, N.J.: Prentice-Hall.

_____ 1965. Reply to Ando and Modigliani and to DePrano and Mayer. *American Economic Review* 55: 753–58.

Friedman, M. and A. Schwartz. 1963. *A Monetary History of the United States 1867–1960*. Princeton: Princeton University Press.

Goldfeld, S.M. and A.S. Blinder. 1972. Some implications of endogenous stabilization policy. *Brookings Papers on Economic Activity* 3: 585–644.

Grenander, V. 1954. On the estimation of regression coefficients in the case of an autocorrelated disturbance. *Annals of Mathematical Statistics* 25: 252–72.

Hall, R.E. 1978. Stochastic implications of the life cycle—permanent income hypothesis: Theory and evidence. *Journal of Political Economy* 86: 971–87.

————— 1981. Intertemporal substitution in consumption. NBER Working Paper No. 720.

Hester, D.E. 1964. Keynes and the quantity theory: A comment on the Friedman–Meiselman CMC paper. *Review of Economics and Statistics* 45: 364–68.

Infante, E.F. and J.L. Stein. 1976. Does fiscal policy matter? *Journal of Monetary Economics* 2: 473–500.

Johnson, H.G. 1971. The Keynesian revolution and the monetary counter-revolution. *American Economic Review* 61: 1–14.

Keran, M. 1976. Monetary policy, balance of payments, and business cycles. *Federal Reserve Bank of St. Louis Review* 49: 7–17.

King, R.G. and C.I. Plosser. 1985. Money, deficits and inflation. In *Understanding Monetary Regimes*. Carnegie–Rochester Series on Public Policy, Vol. 22.

Kochin, L. 1974. Are future taxes anticipated by customers? *Journal of Money, Credit, and Banking* 6: 385–94.

Kormendi, R.C. 1983. Government debt, government spending and private sector behavior. *American Economic Review* 73: 954–1010.

Kotlikoff, L.J. 1984. Taxation and savings: A neo-classical perspective. *Journal of Economic Literature* 22: 4.

Lucas, R.E. 1984. Money in a theory of finance. In *Essays on Macroeconomic Implications of Financial and Labor Markets and Political Process*. Carnegie–Rochester Conference Series on Public Policy, Vol. 21, 9–45.

Mankiw, N.G. and L.H. Summers. 1984. Are tax cuts really expansionary? NBER Working Paper Series.

Mascaro, A. and A.H. Meltzer. 1983. Long- and short-term interest rates in a risky world. *Journal of Monetary Economics* 12: 485–518.

McCallum, B.T. 1981. Monetarist principals and the money stock growth rule. *American Economic Review* 71: 134–38.

————— 1984. Are bond-financed deficits inflationary? A Ricardian analysis. *Journal of Political Economy* 92: 123–35.

Meese, R.A. and K.J. Singleton. 1982. On unit roots and the empirical modelling of exchange rates. *Journal of Finance* 57: 1029–35.

Meltzer, A.H. 1981. Keynes' general theory: A different perspective. *Journal of Economic Literature* 19: 34–64.

Meltzer, A.H. and S.F. Richard. 1985. Why the social security system is in crisis. Unpublished manuscript.

Miller, M.H. and C.W. Upton. 1974. *Macroeconomics: A Neoclassical Introduction*. Homewood, Ill.: Richard D. Irwin.

Modigliani, F.I. 1977. The monetarist controversy or, should we foresake stabilization policies? *American Economic Review* 67: 1–19.

Nelson, C.R. and C.I. Plosser. 1982. Trends and random walks in macroeconomic time series. *Journal of Monetary Economics* 10: 139–62.

Plosser, C.I. 1982. Government financing decisions and asset returns. *Journal of Monetary Economics* 9: 315–52.

————— 1984. Money in a theory of finance. In *Essays on Macroeconomic Implications of Financial and Labor Markets and Political Processes*. Carnegie–Rochester Conference Series on Public Policy, Vol. 21, 47–55.

Plosser, C.I. and G.W. Schwert. 1978. Money, income and sunspots: Measuring economic relationships and the effects of differencing. *Journal of Monetary Economics* 4: 637–60.

Policies to Combat Depressions. 1956. A Conference of the Universities–National Bureau Committee for Economic Research. Princeton: Princeton University Press.

Sargent, T.J. and N. Wallace. 1982. Some unpleasant monetarist arithmetic. *Federal Reserve Bank of Minneapolis Quarterly Review* 6: 1-17.

Seltzer, L.H. 1945. Is a rise in interest rates desirable or inevitable? *American Economic Review* 35.

Silber, W.L. 1970. Fiscal policy in IS-LM analysis: A correction. *Journal of Money, Credit, and Banking* 2: 461–72.

Stulz, R.M. and W. Wasserfallen. 1985. Macroeconomic time series, business cycles and macroeconomic policies. In *Carnegie–Rochester Conference Series on Public Policy*, Vol. 22.

Supplement to Review of Economics and Statistics. 1963. A Conference of the Universities–National Bureau Committee for Economic Research. Conference on Monetary Theory.

Tanner, J.E. 1970. Empirical evidence on the short-run real balance effect in Canada. *Journal of Money, Credit, and Banking* 2: 473–85.

Tinbergen, J. 1952. *On the Theory of Economic Policy.* Amsterdam: North-Holland.

Tobin, J. 1980. *Asset Accumulation and Economic Activity: Reflections on Contemporary Macroeconomic Theory.* Chicago: University of Chicago Press.

———— 1981. The monetarist counter-revolution today—An appraisal. *Economic Journal* 91: 29–42.

Wasserfallen, W. 1985. Makro okonomische Unterschuger mit Rationalen Erwartungen: Empirische Analysen fur die Schweitz. Habilitation thesis accepted by University of Bern. To be published.

Weil, P. 1984. Love thy children: Reflections on the Barro debt neutrality theorem. Harvard University Working Paper.

4

Ruminations on Karl Brunner's Reflections

Alan S. Blinder
PRINCETON UNIVERSITY

1. Introduction

Karl Brunner's mammoth paper is a wide-ranging and detailed survey and evaluation of many issues that are tied in one way or another to the fiscal versus monetary policy debate. It is the kind of paper that overwhelms a discussant by its size and scope. So, to keep my task manageable, I will be selective and not try to touch every base that Karl touches. Still, that will leave me with plenty to do.

The organizers of this conference must have known that the only way to get me to raise my output above its natural rate was to hit me with a series of unanticipated shocks. This they did—with Karl's help. Originally, I was asked to be a discussant of a paper on the evolution of *monetarism* written by the man who invented the word. That sounded interesting. Then came the first unanticipated shock: I was told that the paper would really be about *fiscal policy*. Somehow that made me anticipate a paper full of Brunner–Meltzer type models with emphasis on asset substitutability and the financial aspects of fiscal operations. When the paper finally arrived (just a few days ago), I received my second unanticipated shock. I never imagined that Karl would try to resurrect the old AM/FM debate, today, in the age of VCRs, digital recordings, and cable TV. But he did!

Ironically, it was just this week that I lectured on the monetarist-Keynesian debate in my graduate course at Princeton. In almost three hours of lecturing, I never once mentioned Friedman and Meiselman, Ando and Modigliani, Andersen and Jordan, Blinder and Solow, Goldfeld and Blinder, or any of the other parties to this debate. Apparently, Karl thinks that my graduate students were shortchanged. So I'd like to redress that first. Then I will turn to issues pertaining to the government budget constraint and to the Reagan–Barro equivalence theorem, where, I am happy to say, our disagreements are quite minor.

2. The Intellectual Setting

But first a brief word about the intellectual setting for this debate. Like McCallum (see Chapter 2), Karl reminisces about the bad old days in which Neanderthal Keynesians roamed the land, spreading the false word that money does not matter. McCallum even dates the Neanderthal period as lasting at least until 1965.

Funny, but I don't remember it that way at all. Maybe I'm just too young. But I started studying economics in 1963–the year the Friedman–Meiselman study was published–and grew up thinking that money mattered quite a lot, even though I was exposed to one Keynesian teacher after another and never saw a live monetarist until Leonall Andersen gave a guest lecture at MIT in 1970. My first college textbook was Paul Samuelson's fifth edition published in 1961, and therefore written in 1960 or 1959, which by 1963 had been widely imitated. As I remember, my young, impressionable mind got the strong impression that money and monetary policy mattered quite a bit.

But Karl and Ben induced me to check my memory. So I dusted off my old Samuelson. Let me read you a few quotations. In Chapter 15, immediately after dismissing the crude quantity theory, Samuelson remarked:

> "Few people are still alive who subscribe to the crude quantity theory, but we should not use its inadequacies to damn the whole idea that money can have important effects on macroeconomic magnitudes. . . . The next few chapters will show how monetary policy does have an important influence on the total of spending." (p. 315)

Then on the very next page, he explained that a "sophisticated quantity theorist" does not believe that velocity is constant but claims instead that controlling the money supply will help to control national income. According to the Samuelson of 1961, "this is in agreement with almost any modern theory of income determination" (p. 316). The last sentence of the chapter entices students to read the next two chapters (on banking and central banking) with the words: "So from every point of view, the discussions in the ensuing chapters . . . are of tremendous importance." (p. 316)

In Chapter 18 Samuelson began the "Synthesis of Monetary Analysis and Income Analysis" with the words "Monetary analysis is seen to fit in well with the modern theory of income determination; the stage is set for stabilization policy—central bank monetary policies and government fiscal policies and government fiscal policies." (p. 366) (Notice who got first billing!) He then proceeded to outline the standard "Keynesian" transmission mechanism by means of interest rates and investment.

My question is a simple and rhetorical one: Can anyone reading this book have come away with the ideas that money is unimportant and monetary policy is impotent?

3. Simple Correlations and Reduced Forms

Up until a few years ago, I used to tell Princeton freshmen the story of how the Neanderthal Keynesians, with their stone-age view that money doesn't matter, were vanquished by the Cro-Magnon monetarists, with their equally silly view that fiscal policy doesn't matter. When I did so, I always put the story in the past tense, on the assumption that the issue was dead and buried. The tone was clearly: Thank God we don't argue about *that* any more.

Now, Karl wants us to exhume the body. Although I'm not sure I have penetrated his methodological discussion, he seems to defend simple reduced forms, or even simpler correlation coefficients, as the "right" way to test one broad class of hypotheses against another. As he puts it:

> The "single equation with single variable" was the appropriate choice for an evaluation of a class of hypotheses seriously presented in textbooks and class teachings [p. 41]. Reliance on the correlation coefficient . . . is quite appropriate for the evaluation of the core-class addressed by Friedman and Meiselman [p. 43].

Let me try to explain what I think Karl means, using as my example the simplest version of the St. Louis equation. Then I'll say why I think he is wrong. Suppose that true model of the economy is Eq. (1) of Karl's paper:

$$Y_t = k + aF_t + bM_t + e_t, \tag{1}$$

where e includes quite a lot of things, some of which are at least partly forecastable. If F, M, and e are all orthogonal random variables, then the variance of Y is

$$\mathrm{Var}(Y) = a^2\mathrm{Var}(F) + b^2\mathrm{Var}(M) + \mathrm{Var}(e). \tag{2}$$

I think Karl wants to say that the "core-class" hypothesis of the Cro-Magnon monetarists was that $b^2\mathrm{Var}(M)$ is much bigger than $a^2\mathrm{Var}(F)$, so that movements of M dominate movements of Y. Conversely, the core of the Neanderthal Keynesian view is that $a^2\mathrm{Var}(F)$ is much larger than $b^2\mathrm{Var}(M)$. With orthogonal data the simple correlation coefficients provide the data needed to discriminate between these two hypotheses, since in this model $r(Y, F)$ is proportional to $a\sigma(F)$, and $r(Y, M)$ is proportional to $b\sigma(M)$. This decomposition of $\mathrm{Var}(Y)$ even makes sense, because a high $r(Y, M)$ and a low $r(Y, F)$ would mean that monetary impulses dominate the movement of Y, and vice versa.

At some level I have sympathy with Karl's methodological point of view, since I do think that an economic model must consist both of a set of equations and a judgment about the nature of the dominant stochastic disturbances. But my sympathy is only skin deep.

One reason is trivial and obvious. If F and M covary in the data, the clean decomposition in (2) cannot be done. There is a *covariance* term that Cro-Magnons can attribute to monetary policy and Neanderthals can attribute to fiscal policy. Nothing in the data will adjudicate this dispute, which is more teleological than logical.

Another problem arises when policy is set *purposefully*. At the risk of some duplication, let me state that point as simply as possible, even though Karl has discussed it at length, modernizing it as I do to account for rational expectations. Goldfeld and I (1972) suggested that M and F are not whimsical random variables but may instead be deliberately manipulated to offset changes in e. If monetary policy fully offsets the expected value of e, then

$$M_t = -(1/b)\, E_{t-1}e_t, \tag{3}$$

and (1) becomes

$$Y_t = k + aF_t + (e_t - E_{t-1}e_t). \tag{4}$$

If forecasts are pretty good, the innovation would have small variance, $r(Y, F)$ would be high, and regression (1) would yield a zero coefficient for M. Hence, Neanderthal Keynesians would be judged correct by Karl's criterion. Both F-M and A-J would have become fiscalists. And all because monetary policy was so effective.

On the other hand, if fiscal policy did the stabilizing and monetary policy was random, the corresponding equations would be

$$F_t = -(1/a)E_{t-1}e_t, \quad (5)$$

$$Y_t = k + bM_t + (e_t - E_{t-1}e_t). \quad (6)$$

Now Y and F would be uncorrelated, whereas Y and M are highly correlated, and a regression of the form (1) would assign a zero coefficient to fiscal policy. These are just the findings of F-M and A-J. Karl would judge the Cro-Magnon monetarists correct because fiscal stabilization was so effective.

But neither conclusion makes sense; neither finding implies that either policy tool is powerless to influence GNP. In (6) we have no way to estimate a and in (4) we have no way to estimate b. In either case, purposeful policy reactions deny the econometrician the information he needs to estimate one of the multipliers.

Surely we all know by now that neither a nor b is zero, that both monetary and fiscal policy are from time to time used purposefully, and that many variables are omitted from (1). So why argue about which of two silly hypotheses is the sillier? I'd rather see the fossils of the FM/AM debate left in the grave.

4. The Government Budget Constraint and Fiscal–Monetary Interactions

I have much more favorable things to say about Karl's excellent discussion of the government budget constraint and the issues it raises. In fact, I think we see eye to eye almost totally—which makes both of us, I think, disagree with McCallum. By the way, I think that when Blinder and Solow agree so closely with Brunner and Meltzer, that's worth noting. Maybe we have hit on some deep truth! My capsule summary of the debate would differ in only minor ways from Karl's. It goes like this.

The paper Solow and I published in 1973 dealt with a simple case of *fixed prices* and *fixed tax rates*. It pointed out and explained the paradoxical result that a rise in government spending is more expansionary in the long run if the ensuing deficits are covered by *issuing bonds* than if they are covered by *printing money*—provided the system is stable under both financial policies. More importantly, perhaps, it showed that the likelihood of instability is far greater under bond financing than under money financing.

Notice that this is bad news for monetarism—not as theory but as *policy*—because the "bond-financed" case is essentially the monetarist policy rule of steady (in this case, zero) money growth.

Though the details of our model left much to be desired, I think these basic findings have proven to be very robust. Brunner and Meltzer and Tobin and Buiter established parallel results in full-employment models with variable prices; Buiter, Pyle and Turnovsky, and others allowed both prices and output to vary. Other extensions opened the economy, allowed more assets, and so on.

None of these earlier contributions, however, dealt in a satisfactory way with rational expectations. Actually, I think it is impossible to do that, except in a totally arbitrary way. Let me explain why.

One problem posed by rational expectations is the Reagan–Barro equivalence theorem. If bonds are just congealed future taxes, then the wealth effects that lie at the heart of this analysis disappear. There is no stability issue because bond financing is just tax financing. And the relevant choice is between money finance and tax finance, not between money and bonds. Karl discusses this extensively and well. But let me defer it for the moment, for I have something else in mind.

In conjunction with any sort of forward-looking expectations, the government budget constraint sets up dynamic constraints across policy choices. To take a not very hypothetical example, suppose the current government raises spending and cuts tax rates, thereby opening up a deficit. Current and future governments are thereby obligated to do some combination of

(a)   raising tax rates
(b)   cutting spending
(c)   printing money
(d)   floating more bonds.

(This latter possibility can last forever only if the conditions for stability under bond finance hold; and they may not.) It is rational for people to know this, therefore, and to expect some combination of these events sometime in the future. But, as Karl points out, who knows when? And who knows which ones the government will choose?

In Barro's hands, rational expectations is interpreted to mean that tax cuts covered by debt today must lead to future tax increases of equal present value. In that case, under a host of other assumptions (see below), we get non-Ricardian equivalence, and current bond-financed tax cuts affect nothing. But that's only one of several possibilities.

Sargent and Wallace (1981) assume that if the economy is unstable under bond financing, the government will ultimately have to resort to *money creation*. Since rational expectations in a frictionless world effectively telescope the future back to the present, they conclude that tight money might be inflationary. But that's only a second possibility.

President Reagan and his crowd had a different form of rational expectations in mind. They argued that taking away the tax revenue today was the way to get spending down tomorrow. So far that idea has not worked very well. But who can say it was not a "rational" expectation, or that it was less rational than Barro's or Sargent and Wallace's.

My view on this issue is very similar to Karl's: who knows what or when? If a government opts for bond financing of deficits, which seems to be the default option (pardon the pun!), and it discovers that it has thereby put the economy on an unstable path, something will definitely have to give. The economy will not zoom off to either positive or negative infinity. *Something* will happen. But what? Sargent and Wallace gave us one possibility; another is that the economy will get a new government; yet another is that institutional changes will take place, altering the structure of the model.

Karl gets this analysis just right, I think. He is also right, in my judgment, to point to the tremendous uncertainty that this must cause in people's minds. When an individual has very diffuse priorities over what long-run government policy will be, it strikes me as plausible that his point estimates of future policy variables may have weak effects on his current decisions—which is just the opposite of what Barro and Sargent and Wallace assume. If this is so, then expectational issues, although deep and weighty, may not be of great empirical importance. I, of course, do not pretend to know that this is the case. I merely raise it as a possibility.

Another problem stems from diversity of expectations across individuals. If Barro thinks that current deficits will eventually lead to massive future taxes, if Sargent thinks they will eventually lead to a huge amount of money creation, and if Reagan thinks they will lead to huge future cuts in spending, and the economy will be stable under pure bond financing, then the economy may not converge to any rational expectations equilibrium at all, as Phelps and others have pointed out.

4.a. Monetization

I'd like to say one thing about the *empirical* aspects of the fiscal–monetary interaction. Following King and Plosser, Karl states that "There is . . . no evidence for a contemporaneous relation between deficit and money creation in the U.S.A." (p. 98) That's what I used to think. But I found otherwise in a paper in this conference series two years ago. Let me try to reconcile the two views.

King and Plosser found no zero-order correlation between deficits and money growth over the 1953–82 period. I did several things differently. I used fiscal-year data and included off-budget items to get a more accurate measure of the budget deficit. I used bank reserves rather than the money supply to look directly at the monetization decision rather than at the money multiplier. And I took care to make the dimensions of variables and their alignment in time consistent with the government budget constraint. Nonetheless, I also found no zero-order correlation between deficits and changes in bank reserves over the 1949–81 fiscal years.

But something quite different, and quite surprising, emerged when I allowed the monetization decision to depend on lagged inflation and lagged growth of real federal purchases: a strong and quite robust empirical relationship between deficits and changes in bank reserves emerged. At least over the 1961–81 period, the deficit was a significant determinant of monetization; but the fraction of the deficit that was monetized fell as either inflation or the growth of federal purchases rose. This empirical regularity survived most of my attempts to get rid of it, including adding other variables, shortening the sample period, differencing (à la Plosser and Schwert), and a Chow test for coefficient shifts.

In the end I changed my beliefs. I now think there is reasonably good evidence that larger deficits typically cause (in the Hume sense, not the Granger sense) faster growth of bank reserves in the United States. However, I should point out that the estimated fraction of the deficit that is monetized is never very large, and it gets negative when lagged inflation is high.

5. Non-Ricardian Equivalence

Before discussing Karl's discussion of Ricardian equivalence, I'd like to say a word about *truth-in-naming*. As we all should know by now, David Ricardo thoroughly discussed what is now called the Ricardian equivalence proposition—and rejected it. That does not mean that the equivalence proposition is false; Ricardo probably also believed in bleeding. But it *does* mean that we should stop calling it *Ricardian*. I propose that we call it the *Reagan–Barro* equivalence proposition.

When it comes to the substance of the issue, I feel relatively comfortable with Karl's discussion. I would have changed the emphasis in some places: for example, I attach more importance to the problem of corner solutions at zero bequests. Especially in a growing economy in which children are, on average, better off than their parents and in which bequests in human form are substantial, I suspect that many optimizers would like to leave a negative bequest but cannot. A tax cut or a rise in social security benefits now, balanced by future taxes on our children, is one way to accomplish this.

Karl correctly characterizes the empirical evidence on the equivalence theorem as quite mixed. And he expresses some surprise that the data are not more decisive, because he finds the Barro–Reagan proposition implausible on a priori grounds. I am also surprised. The Barro–Reagan view has proven much harder to reject than I thought. The evidence adduced to date really is too mixed and, as previously noted, too ideologically correlated to resolve the issue.

In fact, a recent paper by Benjamin, Kochin, and Meador suggests that many of the empirical tests of equivalence may be entirely beside the point. Their basic argument is consistent with Barro's work on optimal debt policy and can be summarized as follows.

Tax rates are not arbitrary but are purposefully manipulated by government to minimize deadweight loss over time. As Barro pointed out, the optimizing government will want to smooth tax rates relative to expenditures. Under certainty, the optimal tax rate is constant through time. But when there is uncertainty, the optimal tax rate will evolve as a random walk, following the current estimate of the present value of expenditures.

One implication of this kind of optimizing behavior, pointed out by Benjamin et al., is that the rational expectations consumption function becomes Keynesian. This is easy to see. The rational expectations consumption function appealed to by Barro is farsighted and forward-looking:

$$C_t = k \left[\sum_{s=0}^{\infty} \frac{{}_tY_{t+s}}{(1+r)^s} - \sum_{s=0}^{\infty} \frac{{}_tT_{t+s}}{(1+r)^s} \right]. \qquad (7)$$

In the Barro–Reagan story, any arbitrary change in current T_t is balanced by changes in the opposite direction in some future ${}_tT_{t+s}$'s of equal present value. Hence, the tax term does not change, and neither does C_t.

But if T_t is a random walk, then current T (not current spending) is the best estimator of any future T_{t+s}. So a rise in T_t will be interpreted by consumers as indicating a rise in the *permanent* levels of government spending and taxation. They will therefore reduce their consumption accordingly. So current taxation will have strong Keynesian effects on current consumption.

Note the strong parallels between this argument and the one I made earlier about St. Louis equations. Both econometric procedures make sense *if the government policy instruments are set whimsically*. But both can give seriously misleading results if the government acts purposefully.

6. Conclusion

In sum, I disagree most emphatically with Karl's attempt to resurrect and legitimize the old reduced form approach, but I agree with most of what he says about the government budget constraint and the non-Ricardian equivalence theorem. Two out of three is not bad!

Since Karl is labeled a monetarist and I am labeled a Keynesian, and since neither one of us shuns our label, maybe this wide-ranging agreement suggests that the labels are *obsolete* and possibly even *dysfunctional*. I, for one, would be happy to declare the monetarist–Keynesian debate over *today, right here in St. Louis*. What an appropriate place!

References

Barro, R. J. 1974. Are government bonds net wealth? *Journal of Political Economy* 82: 1095–1117.

Benjamin, D. K., L. Kochin, and M. Meador. n.d. Observational equivalence of rational and irrational consumers if taxation is efficient. Unpublished manuscript.

Blinder, A. S. and R. M. Solow. 1973. Does fiscal policy matter? *Journal of Public Economics* 2: 319–37.

Brunner, K. and A. H. Meltzer. 1976. An aggregative theory for a closed economy. In *Monetarism*, ed., J. Stein. Amsterdam: North-Holland.

Buiter, W. 1976. Capacity constraints, government financing and the short-run and long-run effects of fiscal policy. Unpublished manuscript.

Friedman, M. and D. Meiselman. 1963. The relative stability of monetary velocity and the investment multiplier in the United States, 1897–1958. In *Stabilization Policies*. Englewood Cliffs, N.J.: Prentice-Hall.

Goldfeld, S. M. and A. S. Blinder. 1972. Some implications of endogenous stabilization policy. *Brookings Papers on Economic Activity* 3: 585–640.

King, R. G. and C. I. Plosser. 1984. Money, deficits and inflation. Presented at Carnegie–Rochester Conference Series on Public Policy.

Pyle, D. H. and S. J. Turnousky. 1976. The dynamics of government policy in an inflationary economy: An 'intermediate run' analysis. *Journal of Money, Credit and Banking* 8: 411–37.

Samuelson, P. A. 1961. *Economics: An Introductory Analysis*. New York: McGraw-Hill.

Sargent, T. J. and N. Wallace. 1981. Some unpleasant monetarist arithmetic. *Federal Reserve Bank of Minneapolis Quarterly Review* 6: 1–17.

Tobin, J. and W. Buiter. 1976. Long run effects of fiscal and monetary policy on aggregate demand. In *Monetarism*, ed. J. Stein. Amsterdam: North-Holland.

5

Comment on Karl Brunner's "Fiscal Policy in Macro Theory: A Survey and Evaluation"

Robert J. Gordon
NORTHWESTERN UNIVERSITY
AND NATIONAL BUREAU OF ECONOMIC RESEARCH

1. Introduction

It is a great pleasure for me to discuss the essay by Karl Brunner; this continues a tradition of discussing each other's work that dates back at least a decade. Much of Brunner's massive survey is admirable, reflecting a deep and careful analysis of central issues in fiscal policy, and the way events have changed perceptions of fiscal policy. The comprehensive and up-to-date reference list adds to the value of the contribution. Because of its length, I cannot delve into every issue raised by Brunner, but I will concentrate on three areas where, I believe, his analysis needs to be qualified and supplemented: (a) the intellectual history of the monetary–fiscal debate; (b) the interpretation of St. Louis equations; and (c) Ricardian equivalence and other theoretical issues.

2. The Interaction of Events and Ideas

Brunner drags up from his dusty shelves of old journals the infamous "battle of the radio stations (AM–FM)" and defends what has long been dismissed—an evaluation of alternative viewpoints with simple correlations between spending and money on the one hand and autonomous spending on the other. The essence of Brunner's defense is that "the 'single equation with single variable' was the appropriate choice for an evaluation of a class of hypotheses seriously presented in textbooks and class teachings."

Most spectators of the AM–FM debate found the single-variable framework unappealing because they could find no example of any influential economist at that time who believed that "only fiscal policy matters," and even if such an economist did exist, he never would have expected to find a stable and constant coefficient of total spending on autonomous spending because the output multiplier was a variable, not a constant, depending on, among other things, a host of changing tax rates. The Andersen–Jordan St. Louis contribution was taken more seriously precisely because its point of departure was a two-variable test of monetary and fiscal policy together.

Brunner begins with intellectual history and then delves into econometric details. Let me begin with my own version of the intellectual history that emphasizes the influence of events (rather than journal debates) on the evolution of ideas. This account is sprinkled with a few quotes to indicate what people actually believed in the 1950s and early 1960s. We then turn to an interpretation of the empirical issues.

The central paradigm of macroeconomics as it emerged from World War II was indeed the Keynesian multiplier theory and its endorsement of an activist fiscal policy to overcome the inherent instability of private investment. Monetary theory lurked in the shadows, discredited at least temporarily as a result of a major event that dominated early postwar ideas— namely the juxtaposition between early 1938 and late 1940 of a weak economic recovery, explosive monetary growth, and a short-term interest rate that was rapid and constant between early 1938 and late 1941, the economy's recovery floundered until military spending began in earnest in late 1940, after which real GNP suddenly jumped by almost 20 percent in a single year. This chronology ingrained a deep-seated belief in the potency of fiscal policy and the "pushing on a string" analogy for monetary policy.

But money was not ignored totally in the late 1940s, and many economists took note of the fact that the quantity of nominal money had tripled between 1940 and 1945. Contemporary accounts displayed a curious inconsistency, with a monetary expansion viewed as impotent but a monetary contraction viewed as too dangerously potent to risk, as in Lawrence Seltzer's (1945) remark that "there is great risk that the deflationary effects of a radical rise in interest rates might be so severe as to throw the whole economy into a crushing depression" (p. 844).

As for the teaching of undergraduates, I have never managed to obtain Samuelson's 1948 first edition, but I do have the 1951 second edition, which, I hasten to add, was not the edition that I used in college but was obtained at a used book sale. Samuelson in 1951, more than a decade before the AM–FM debate, does not reveal himself as a hard-line "only fiscal policy matters" guy. Instead, his treatment reflects the uncomfortable asymmetry of early postwar Keynesian ideas. There are over 25 index entries for money and monetary policy and another 20 for the interest rate. On page 342 are listed as effects of a $1 billion open-market purchase:

> the general easing of interest rates and the increased availiability of credit to would-be investors, . . . the upward shift in the earlier chapters' investment-income schedule resulting from the lowered rate of interest, . . . the primary and secondary increases in income resulting from the increased flow of investment, . . . and the increased stock of buildings, equipment, and inventories that will later result from the cumulation of a high rate of investment.

In typical late 1940s style, this account is immediately followed by three qualifications that make monetary policy "at best a supplement to other stabilization policies, such as fiscal policy." The three qualifications are these: (1) "Changes in the amount of money may have very weak effects on the rate of interest if rates are already very low." (2) "Even if there are some changes in the rate of interest, the rate of investment spending may turn out to be relatively little affected by changes in interest rates. The prospects for invesement may depend much more on the depressed state of business." (3) "The Central Banker may be unwilling to push monetary policy very far." Clearly the first two qualifications reflected events of the late 1930s, and the third the Fed's pegging of interest rates in this pre-Accord edition of the textbook. The late 1940s asymmetry is implicit in the assumption that the problem of monetary policy is pumping up a depressed economy rather than slowing down an overheated one.

Over the following decade there was a gradual but continuous shift of opinion toward an increased role for monetary policy, marked by mileposts including the Patman Committee Inquiry, the negative reaction of many economists to the downgrading of money in the Radcliffe report, and the influence of the monetary research of Milton Friedman, his students, and others. The growing belief in the importance of money can be traced to several episodes in the first postwar decade. Those who believed that the large outstanding stock of public debt prevented effective monetary action and required the pegging of interest rates either lost credibility or changed their opinions when the higher interest rates that followed the Treasury–Fed Accord failed to have any disastrous consequences for debt management or the economy's performance in general. The relative mildness of the 1954 recession was due partly to countercyclical monetary policy and helped to lessen the belief that monetary policy was only effective in countering inflation and suffered from an asymmetric impotence in dealing with slack demand. The continued acceleration of inflation despite rising interest rates in 1956–57 tempered the belief that monetary policy had unique curative powers to combat inflation. By 1962 Harry Johnson was able to observe that "the wheel has come full circle, and pre-

vailing opinion has returned to the characteristic 1920s view that monetary policy is probably more effective in checking deflation than in checking inflation." Although Johnson may have been ahead of his time,
influenced as he was by monetary research at the University of Chicago,
nevertheless his account provides a picture far from Brunner's, with the
"hard-line fiscalists" hard to find.

Turning now to more contemporary quotes—I seem to have saved my
final exam in Economics 1 at Harvard, taken in May 1959—I find interesting evidence to support the idea of "fiscal dominance," but I find no evidence at all of the influence of Brunner's "hard-line fiscalists" believing
"money doesn't matter." Fiscal dominance is reflected in the fact that the
first half of the exam consisted of two questions: one hour on fiscal policy
and a half hour on monetary policy. Inspection of the four-part fiscal
policy question makes one scoff in retrospect at the idea of regressing
aggregate spending on autonomous spending, because 1959 Harvard
undergraduates were supposed to know that the multiplier effect of a
change in government spending depended on whether or not the spending
was financed by increased taxes, and they were given the option of concluding that an increase in spending accompanied by an equal increase in
taxes might raise unemployment or leave it unchanged. The half-hour
monetary question reflected not a ritual belief that "money doesn't
matter," but rather the same old asymmetry. To quote the question, "It is
frequently argued that monetary policy is effective in controlling inflation,
but less successful in fighting unemployment. Trace the mechanism
through which the tools of monetary policy operate under alternative cyclical conditions, and comment on their effectiveness."

Returning to the influence of events, the AM–FM debate coincided
with the heyday of activist fiscal policy, dubbed the "new economics." By
then, changes in government spending were recognized to involve gesta-
tion lags and to have allocative side effects, and so the central policy tool
had become changes in income tax rates, which of course involves
changes in the spending multiplier rather than a stable multiplier, as in
Brunner's caricature of fiscalism. Although the consensus policy paradigm of 1965 did not neglect monetary policy nor deny that monetary
tightness could interfere with the pace of economic expansion, monetary
policy was basically kept in the background and relegated to the role of
maintaining a low and stable level of long-term interest rates to foster the
goal of stimulating long-term economic growth.

This policy framework collapsed with amazing speed after 1967 as the
result of the interaction of events and economic writings. My graduate
school classmates and I were acutely aware of the timing of this turn in
the intellectual tide, as we began our first teaching jobs in the fall of 1967
and almost immediately found our graduate school education incapable

of explaining the evolution of the economy. The most important ingredient in this revolution was the Friedman–Phelps "natural rate hypothesis," the role of which is well known and not our subject today. More relevant was the blow struck by Andersen and Jordan in 1968. Although activist advocates eventually regrouped and presented convincing evidence of fatal statistical flaws in the St. Louis procedure, particularly the contribution of Goldfeld and Blinder, their disarray lasted long enough to partially discredit fiscal activism. To add to the overall indictment of fiscal policy provided by the St. Louis equation, Robert Eisner in 1969 made an important attack on the efficacy of the temporary tax changes favored by mid-1960s policy activists. Using the framework of Friedman's permanent income hypothesis of consumption, Eisner argued that a temporary income tax cut or surcharge would fail to alter permanent income and thus would have a lower spending multiplier. Further, the lag in the effect of fiscal policy might be long and/or unpredictable, with the length of the lag depending on the public's subjective assessment of the likelihood that the tax change soon would be reversed.

These academic criticisms of the activist case might not have been so persuasive if they had not been accompanied by supporting events. The dramatic drop in the personal saving rate in late 1968 and the failure of spending growth to slow appreciably in response to the temporary tax surcharge was consistent both with the St. Louis claim that monetary multipliers had previously been underestimated and fiscal multipliers overestimated and with the Eisner critique. Blinder's retrospective econometric evidence of this period shows that temporary tax changes are not completely ineffective, but their multiplier impact may be as little as one-half of tax changes regarded as permanent, and the effect on consumption of any tax change may take several years to occur.

3. Empirical Issues in St. Louis Equations

The empirical issues involved in the AM–FM debate and subsequent St. Louis equation are so well known that little time need be spent reviewing them. The St. Louis equation represented an advance over Friedman and Meiselman in three main dimensions: testing the effects of monetary and fiscal policy in the same equation, using full employment instead of actual government spending and revenues, and expressing variables in first differences. However, the St. Louis reduced form was vulnerable to the central criticism that coefficients of both the monetary and fiscal policy variables were biased if there were any correlation between either policy variable and the error term in the equation, representing the whole panoply of omitted demand and supply shocks that drove changes in aggregate demand.

The general case for this point was best expressed by Goldfeld and Blinder, and once their case was stated, everyone understood the argument that the monetary policy coefficients were biased upward, since during all of the original Andersen–Jordan sample period the Fed was acting to stabilize interest rates rather than money, thus creating a passive positive response of money to any demand shocks in either the money or commodity markets. And there was no surprise when Ando and Modigliani reported their experiment that, when estimated to artificial data generated by the MPS model, the Andersen–Jordan technique substantially overstated monetary effects and understated fiscal effects. But this still left open the source of the fiscal bias. If a downward bias on fiscal policy coefficients in the St. Louis equation occurs because active fiscal policy has been pursued within the sample period, thus creating a negative correlation between government spending and the error term, what were these episodes when fiscal activism was so effective? In two published comments (1971, 1976), I pointed to the set of events in the Eisenhower administration that led to this result.

Most important, there was a huge negative correlation between the decline in defense spending that took place between 1953 and 1956, and the (dare I say) autonomous bursts of automobile spending associated with new models in 1955 and export spending partly associated with the Suez crisis in 1956. (With reference to McCallum's paper in this volume, it is important to note that this negative relationship displays a positive serial correlation extending over two years.) I recall Paul Samuelson's injunction to us fledgling graduate students in the mid-1960s that he would flunk anyone who produced an econometric explanation of the high level of auto sales in 1955. I later told the story, to explain the Andersen–Jordan result in terms of efficacious fiscal policy, that "President Eisenhower had decided to stop the Korean war in 1953 because he could see the 1955 auto boom and 1956 Suez crisis coming, and he wanted to get defense spending out of the way to avoid overheating the economy." What is not facetious is the remarkable record of the Eisenhower administration in the 1958 recession in creating a time path for nondefense government purchases that rose as the economy fell and fell as the economy recovered. In my comment (1976) I showed, by alternatively including and excluding a proxy for autonomous spending from a St. Louis equation, that in the Eisenhower period fiscal coefficients were low and downward biased, in the Nixon–Ford period they were high and upward biased as a result of procyclical fiscal policy, and in the Kennedy–Johnson era they were in between. The original St. Louis equation was dominated by the Eisenhower sample period and by the negative correlation between the post-Korean decline in defense spending and the mid-1950s business expansion.

Viewing this whole literature from the mid-1980s, we find naive the entire literature on "autonomous spending," because (as McCallum's paper suggests) nothing is truly autonomous. Recent papers have more fruitfully viewed business cycles as being generated by "innovations" in both financial and real variables, where "innovation" is defined as the error in an equation that relates the variable in question to its own past values and the past values of everything else. In this context I have recently completed a research project that reexamines the behavior of household and business investments in newly created quarterly data extending back to 1919 [see Gordon and Veitch (1984)]. Strong evidence is provided to support both sides of the AM–FM debate, for innovations in the money supply have a substantial influence on both household and business investments, but there is still room for a major impact on the business cycle of autonomous innovations in structures investments (both residential and nonresidential).

4. Ricardian Equivalence and Other Issues

The rest of Brunner's paper is more satisfactory. There is a sensible discussion of "intergenerational altruism" and "intergenerational selfishness" in the context of the Barro–Ricardo equivalence theory. As a matter of historical record, I wish that Brunner had cited Patinkin's incorporation into macroeconomic analysis of a variable proportion (k) of outstanding government bonds treated as net private wealth. Patinkin's treatment anticipated many of the implications of Barro's analysis without taking any position over whether k is at an extreme value of zero, as assumed by Barro, or unity, as assumed in some traditional Keynesian analysis.

Brunner recognizes that "the context of risk could explain ... the appearance of bequest without a bequest motive [as] formalized by Barro." Risk, however, is just one of the reasons why I was never convinced by the Barro logic, however dutifully I continue to teach it in the graduate school classroom. As one without children and likely to leave a substantial bequest, it immediately became evident that there is a more important reason than risk to explain why individuals often leave bequests without any necessary altruism for future generations. After all, we are supposed to be able to insure ourselves against risk by buying annuities. But a more important additional set of factors—high transactions costs and inconvenience, as well as imperfect capital markets—make it almost impossible for a well-off person to "go out" with a zero net worth. There is no rental market for the type of house I live in, so in order to buy an annuity with all my assets, I would have to move. Renting a car is expensive, and renting my personal library of books and journals would be impossible. People like me are likely to behave according to a permanent income theory of the flow of consumption services and to leave whatever assets are necessary to maintain that flow of services to worthy charities. Since my heirs are likely to be nonprofit and nontaxable organizations, there is simply no present value of future tax liabilities to consider, and the Barro theorem falls to the ground. The Reagan tax cuts financed by deficit spending have made me feel good, and I have spent some of the proceeds.

Of course, I have not spent all of the proceeds, because simultaneously there have been substantial increases in Keogh and IRA ceilings that have induced me to save more as well. This tug of war between conflicting incentives bears on the empirical evidence "on the Ricardian theme" reviewed at such length in Brunner's paper. Reduced-form equations can be useful, and I have estimated plenty of them in my work on inflation and, more recently, on investment. But the equations of Feldstein–Kormendi type, summarized by Brunner, seem unlikely to provide any reliable evidence of the issues at hand. First, the inclusion of government spending and tax revenues as explanatory variables in a consumption equation runs afoul of the Goldfeld–Blinder critique for the same reasons as does the St. Louis equation. Second, the tax schedule is progressive, and if people in different tax brackets have different propensities to consume, the schedule relating total consumption to total tax revenue will be nonlinear. Third, the lags that Blinder found between changes in taxes and changes in spending are neglected. Fourth, no distinction is made between temporary and permanent tax changes. Fifth, tax law changes that alter disposable income, like a neutral surcharge, can have totally different effects than legislative changes that twist the incentives to consume and to save, as in my IRA–Keogh example. Surely Brunner is aware of all this, so I wonder why he takes all this empirical work so seriously.

5. Concluding Remarks

Bunner's paper treats numerous other issues that do not appear to require comment here. I would enter only two qualifications. First, Brunner's long and sensitive discussion of the Sargent–Wallace deficit analysis is slightly marred from his uncriticial analysis of the Mankiw–Summers paper on consumption and money demand. There are at least three problems with that paper that shed doubt on its credibility: (a) the implausible assumption that the responsiveness of money demand to changes in investment is zero; (b) the lack of evidence for the postwar period of any difference in the fit of GNP and consumption when entered into a money demand equation with a flexible lag structure [see Gordon (1984)]; and (c) the awkward fact that a larger share of demand deposits is held by business firms than by households. Mankiw and Summers do not make a convincing case that would support contractionary effects of tax cuts.

The second qualification refers to Barro's tax smoothing hypothesis on the behavior of deficits. Although somewhat skeptical of the empirical robustness of Barro's approach, Brunner calls it "the only game in town." Yet a paper by Barro (1984) that Brunner does not cite was dismissed at a recent conference as being unsuccessful both on theoretical and empirical grounds. As one discussant asked, "How is it that policymakers in Washington figured out the Ramsey optimal tax rule 50 years before public finance economists?" Consider social security, for which tax smoothing means full actuarial funding of the expected program of benefits. And the theory fails empirically, because the coefficient in a debt change equation on temporary government spending is zero rather than unity as required by the theory, and the World War II years have to be thrown out.

A concluding comment is that, given the length of Brunner's present paper, the attention given to reduced-form empirical evidence on various issues seems excessive. Other, perhaps more interesting, issues regarding fiscal policy might have been covered instead. He might have reconsidered the effects of changes in the monetary–fiscal policy mix on real interest rates and the exchange rate, with and without Ricardian equivalence. Was the shift in the policy mix with the ensuing appreciation of the dollar the real key to the extent of disinflation; if so, what are the theoretical arguments for reversing the mix to avoid future deficits or for maintaining the mix to hold the benefits of disinflation? What are the implications of tax reform for macro theory, particularly a shift to base broadening with lower marginal rates, or a shift to a broad-base progressive consumption tax? What are the implications of current large government deficits for the public choice idea that the best way to reduce government spending is to reduce tax rates—this just hasn't happened when defense spending is included. Overall, I cannot help feeling that the empirical work examined is too flimsy to merit so much attention from this fine theorist, and I cannot help wishing that a paper on fiscal policy in macro theory had contained more about theory.

References

Barro, Robert J. 1984. The behavior of U. S. deficits. NBER Working Paper 1309. March. In *The American Business Cycle: Continuity and Change*, ed. R.J. Gordon. Chicago: University of Chicago Press. Forthcoming.

Eisner, Robert. 1969. Fiscal and monetary policy reconsidered. *American Economic Review* 59: 897–905.

Gordon, Robert J. 1971. Notes on money, income, and Gramlich. *Journal of Money, Credit, and Banking* 3: 533–45.

_____ 1976. Perspectives on monetarism. In *Monetarism*, ed. J. Stein, pp. 52–66. Amsterdam: North–Holland.

_____ 1984. The 1981–82 velocity decline: A structural shift in income or money demand? In *Conference on Monetary Targeting and Velocity*, pp. 67–99. Federal Reserve Bank of San Francisco.

_____ ed. n.d. *The American Business Cycle: Continuity and Change*. University of Chicago Press. Forthcoming.

Gordon, Robert J. and John M. Veitch. 1984. Fixed investment in the American business cycle, 1919–83. In *The American Business Cycle: Continuity and Change*, ed. R.J. Gordon. Chicago: University of Chicago Press. Forthcoming.

Johnson, Harry G. 1962. Monetary theory and policy. *American Economic Review* 52: 335–84.

Patinkin, Don. 1965. *Money, Interest, and Prices*, 2d ed. New York: Harper & Row.

Seltzer, Lawrence H. 1945. Is a rise in interest rates desirable or inevitable? *American Economic Review* 35: 831–50.

Part III

PROSPECTS FOR POLICY ACTIVISM

6

Can Policy Activism Succeed?
A Public Choice Perspective

James M. Buchanan
CENTER FOR STUDY OF PUBLIC CHOICE
GEORGE MASON UNIVERSITY

1. Introduction

The question posed in the title assigned to me presupposes the existence
of an ordering of options along some scale of presumably agreed-on pre-
ferredness or desirability. Only if this presupposition is made does it
become appropriate to ask whether or not politics, as it operates, can be
expected to select the most preferred option on the ordering, or, less
ambitiously, to select, on average, options that would allow the pattern or
sequence of "choices" to be adjudged "successful." The generalized
public-choice answer to the question, given the required presupposition, is
reasonably straightforward, and it is essentially that of classical political
economy. Those who make political decisions can be expected to choose
in accordance with agreed-on or "public interest" norms only if the institutional structure is such as to make these norms coincident with those of
"private interest." The public chooser, whether voter, aspiring or elected
politician, or bureaucrat, is no different in this role than in other roles,
and if incentives are such that the coincidence of interest is absent, there
will be no "successful" political ordering over the feasible options. I shall
return to the possible coincidence of interest following Section 2.

The more fundamental question to be asked, however, involves the
appropriateness of the required presupposition—that concerning the possibility of any meaningful ordering of policy options, quite independently
of any problems of implementation. This question has been obscured
rather than clarified by those economists who resort to "social welfare
functions." These functions impose a totally artificial and meaningless
ordering on "social states" without offering any assistance toward facilitat-

ing choice from among the set of options feasibly available to the public chooser. Section 2 examines this fundamental question in the context of the issues that prompted the assigned title.

2. Is It Possible to Define an Ordering of Policy Options Along an Agreed-on "Success" Scalar?

In this section I propose to ignore totally all problems of policy implementation—all public choice problems, if you will. For simplicity, assume the existence of a genuinely benevolent despot, who sincerely seeks to do that which is "best" for all of those who are members of the political–economic–social community. How can we describe the utility function of this despot? It is easy, of course, to list several desired end-states. Full employment, stable and predictable value in the monetary unit, high and sustainable rates of economic growth, stable international order—these may be mutually agreed-on objectives for policy action. But there may be conflict among the separate objectives (to raise a topic of much debate–discussion of the 1950s that has been relatively neglected in the 1980s). How are we to model the trade-offs among the objectives within the utility function of the benevolent despot, if indeed such conflicts should arise?

I presume that the despot can act so as to influence macroeconomic variables in the economy; I leave possible rational expectations feedbacks to the other paper in this session. But how "should" the despot act, and, in this model, how "will" he act? There is no definitive answer to these questions until and unless the utility function is defined more fully.

There is, of course, an empty response to the question posed in the title to this section. Clearly, if the despot can, by our presumption, influence macroeconomic variables by policy action, then, by some criterion of his own, he can be "successful." But presumably we seek to employ a more objective criterion for success, one that can at least conceptually be observed by others than the despot himself.

For simplicity, let us assume that the despot is concerned only about domestic employment and monetary stability; we ignore all nondomestic considerations, and we put aside problems of growth. Further, let us restrict attention to standard macropolicy tools. The despot here is assumed to be unable, at least in the time frame of the policy under consideration, to modify the structural features of the economy. With these simplifications, we can go further and specify the objective function more precisely. Let us assume that the despot seeks to guarantee that level of employment that is consistent with stability in the value of the monetary unit, given the institutional structure of the economy. The objective reduces to a single price level target.

Even in this highly restricted setting, which is by no means that which might command consensus as a normative posture, the despot cannot simply "choose" the ultimate end objective from an available set of options. That is to say, "stability in the value of the monetary unit" cannot be selected as if from off a policy shelf. The despot is further restricted by the tools of policy available, which in this setting are those of the familiar fiscal (budgetary) and monetary instruments. Nominal demand can be increased, directly or indirectly, or reduced, directly or indirectly, by the use of fiscal–monetary tools, either separately or in some mix. Even if we ignore, as indicated, the expectational-induced feedbacks generated by resort to any instrument, there remains the task of predicting accurately the relationship between the instrument, economic structure, and ultimate objective. The structural features of the economy are not invariant over time, and a policy thrust that might be successful under one set of conditions, say in t_0, may fail, say, in t_1, because of structural shifts. At best, therefore, the truly benevolent despot can only be partially successful, even given the most clearly defined target for policy.

3. Monolithic and Nonbenevolent Despot

The presumption of benevolence on the part of political agents is not, of course, acceptable within a public-choice perspective. It is precisely this presumption that has been a central focus of the overall public-choice critique of the theory of economic policy. Political agents must be presumed to maximize personal utilities in a behavioral model that is invariant, as between public and private roles or capacities. The structure of decision making may, however, affect utility-maximizing behavior through shifts in the effective constraints on choice.

In this section, I shall discuss briefly the simplest possible decision structure, one in which political decisions are lodged within a single monolithic authority (in the limit in one person) which (who) is not directly accountable to or subject to constituency pressures, whether or not these be explicitly "democratic" (electoral) in nature. In this model, it is evident, quite apart from any historical record, that the despot will find it advantageous to resort to money creation over and beyond any amount that might characterize the "ideal" behavior of the benevolent counterpart considered above. This result emerges, quite simply, because incentive effects must be taken into account, and the despot, even if totally immune from constituency pressures, must reckon with individual adjustments to alternative revenue-generating instruments. Through a policy of revenue-maximizing inflation, defined in a dynamic sense, the despot can extract the full value of monetary structure (that is, the value differential between a monetary structure and a barter structure).[1]

The amount of revenue that may be potentially raised through money creation is, of course, finite. And the totally uncontrolled despot may seek to utilize the taxing and debt-issue power over and beyond the inflationary revenue limits. The precise features of the despot's policy mix will depend, in part, on his time horizon in relation to the behavioral reactions of the population. These features need not be examined in detail here. It is sufficient, for my purposes, to conclude that the monolithic despot will be successful only in terms of his own criteria, and that by any of the more familiar criteria for policy success, the failure would be manifest.

4. Monolithic and Nonbenevolent Agent Subject to Electoral Constraints

The analysis becomes more complex once we introduce electoral feedback constraints on the behavior of the monolithic political agent. Assume now that decision authority remains concentrated, but that the holder of this authority is subject to potential electoral replacement at designated periodic intervals. In this model the "governor" cannot expect to use his authority for personal enrichment for any extended period. Under some conditions, simple wealth-maximizing strategy might involve revenue-maximizing exploitation during the period of office, with no attention to possible reelection. In other conditions, the wealth-maximizing strategy might involve the effort to remain in office, in which case, short-run revenue maximization via inflation, debt creation, and taxation will be mitigated. If the agent is modeled as a simple revenue maximizer, it seems unlikely that his pattern of behavior would be adjudged "successful" by external criteria under either of these circumstances.

The more interesting model is one in which the agent is motivated by other considerations than wealth, the simplest model being that in which political position is itself the single maximand. The agent's behavior will, in this case, be constrained by expectations of electoral support. The question then becomes one of determining to what extent voters, generally, or in a required winning coalition, will support or oppose patterns of policy outcomes that might be deemed "successful" by external criteria. Given the postulated motivation here, the agent will base behavior strictly on constituency response.

Consider this question in the terms introduced earlier, that of a unique objective of monetary stability. Will a sufficiently large voting constituency support a regime that seeks only this policy objective? This question may be examined in the calculus of the individual voter or potential voter.

Two separate difficulties arise. The first involves the absence of individual voter responsibility for electoral outcomes in large-number constituencies. Even if the individual knows that the agent elected is fully responsive to the electoral process, because he knows that his own voting choice will rarely, if ever, be decisive, the individual may not vote. And if he does vote, he has little or no incentive to become informed about the alternatives. And if he votes, and even if he is reasonably well informed, there is little or no incentive for him to vote his "interests" rather than his "whims." Hence, there is only a remote linkage between what might be defined by the observing external "expert" as the "interest" of the voters and the support that is given to a prospective political agent who promises these externally defined "interests." This difficulty alone suggests that political agents cannot be "held responsible" by the electoral process nearly to the extent that is suggested by naive models of electoral feedback.

A second difficulty emerges even when the first is totally ignored. Even if all individuals are somehow motivated to vote and to do so in terms of their well-considered interests, these interests will not be identical for all voters. There are differentials among persons in the relative benefits and costs of any macropolicy action. Even the ideally responsive political agent will meet only the demands of the relevant coalition of voters, as determined by the precise voting rules.

Consider a single political agent who must satisfy a simple majority of constituency voters. If voters' interests in the employment–inflation trade-off can be presumed to be single peaked, the political agent's optimal strategy requires satisfying the median voter. It seems likely that this median voter will tend to be *myopic* in his behavior in the electoral process. He will place an unduly high value on the short-term benefits of enhancing employment relative to the long-term, and possibly permanent, costs of inflation. He will do so because, as a currently decisive voter, he can insure the capture of *some* benefits in the immediate future. By foregoing such short-term benefits in a "rational" consideration of the long-term costs, the currently decisive voter *cannot* guarantee against the incurrence of such long-term costs in future periods. This asymmetrical result follows from the potential shiftability of majority voting coalitions. A subsequent period may allow a different median voter or coalition of voters to emerge as dominant—a decisive voter or group that may choose to inflate from strictly short-term considerations. To the extent that this takes place, all of the initial benefits of policy prudence may be offset. In the recognition of this prospect, why should the decisive voter or coalition of voters in the initial period exhibit nonmyopic "rationality" in the sense indicated?[2]

The ultimate answer to the assigned question is clear in this highly simplified model for "democratic" politics. Policy activism cannot be successful if the criterion of success is long-term monetary stability, a criterion that seems most likely to emerge consensually in a constitutional process of deliberation.[3]

5. Nonmonolithic and Nonbenevolent Agents in a Political Structure Subject to Varying Electoral Constraints

The political models examined in sections 3 and 4 were oversimplified in the assumption that authority was placed in a single agent or agency. As we approach reality, it is necessary to recognize that policy-making authority is likely to be divided among several agents or agencies, who (which) may be subjected to quite different electoral controls or constraints and, hence, potentially affected by differing electoral pressures. For example, fiscal or budgetary policies may be made in a wholly different process, institutionally, from monetary policy, and, even within the institutional structure of budgetary policy, authority may be divided between executive and legislative branches of government, subjected to varying electoral constraints, as defined by such things as breadth of constituencies, length of terms of office, voting structure within agency (in legislatures and committees), legally defined responsibilities, and so on.

The direction of difference in effects between this more realistic political model and the monolithic model previously examined seems evident. To the extent that policy-making authority is divided, the proclivity toward response to short-term pressures is increased. Any array of results along the success criterion indicated would indicate that the divided-authority model ranks well below its monolithic counterpart.

6. Nonbenevolent but Monolithic Agent Divorced from Direct Electoral Constraints but Subject to Legal–Constitutional Rules against Personal Enrichment

If there is little or no basis for expecting political agents to express benevolence in their policy behavior, and if, as suggested, the standard "democratic" controls will not themselves insure patterns of outcomes that meet reasonable criteria of success, alternative institutional structures must be analyzed. Consider, first, a model in which decision-making authority is lodged in a single agent or agency and one that is specifically divorced from the electoral process—an agent or agency that does not face continual electoral checks. To prevent that potential for excess under the model discussed in section 3, however, suppose that the agent or members of the agency are placed within enforcible legal–constitutional limits with reference to his or their personal or private enrichment, either directly or indirectly. That is to say, the agent or members of the agency cannot use the money creation and/or taxing power to finance their own private consumption needs or accumulation (e.g., Swiss bank accounts) desires. Beyond this restriction, however, we shall assume that the agent or members of the agency is (are) not limited in behavior except in the overall and general mandate to carry out "good" macroeconomic policy.

This model can, of course, be recognized as one that is closely analogous to the monetary authority of the Federal Reserve Board in the United States. Some elements of the model discussed in section 3—that of the nonconstrained despot—describe the existing structure, and, more importantly, some political controls are exercised; but, for my purposes, the existing monetary authority fits the model reasonably well.

The problem becomes one of predicting the behavior of such an agent and of assessing this behavior in terms of the success criterion introduced. Neither economic nor public-choice analysis is capable of being of much assistance in this respect. To make a prediction, one must get inside the utility function of the agent (or of those who participate in agency decisions). In particular, it would be necessary to know something about the internal rate of time preference that will characterize behavior. If, as we have assumed, demand-enhancing action is known to generate short-term benefits at the expense of long-term costs, the behavior of the monopolistic and discretionary agent in making this trade-off will depend strictly on his own, private, rate of time preference, as expressed "for" the community. That is to say, under the conditions indicated, the agent will not, personally, secure the benefits or suffer the costs. By definition, the agent is not *responsible*, in the sense of a reward–penalty calculus.

This absence of responsibility itself suggests that the behavior of the discretionary agent is likely to be less carefully considered, to be based on less information, and hence to be more erratic than would be the case under some alternative reward–penalty structure. The model further suggests that the agent here is more likely to be responsive to the passing whims of intellectual-media "fashion" than might be the case in the presence of some residual claimancy status. To the extent that the agent is at all responsive to interest-group pressures, such response seems likely to be biased toward those groups seeking near-term benefits and biased against those groups that might be concerned about long-term costs, if for no other reason than the difference in temporal dimension itself. Organized pressures for the promotion of short-term benefits exist while there may be no offsetting organization of long-term interests. This bias might well be exaggerated if the agent or agency is assigned functions that cause the development of relationships with particular functional groups in the policy (e.g., banking and finance). In sum, although there is really no satisfactory predictive model for behavior of the genuinely discretionary agent or agency, there are plausibly acceptable reasons to suggest that policy failures will tend to take the directions indicated in the discussion here.

Viewed in this perspective, and in application to the Federal Reserve agency in the United States, and perhaps notably after the removal of international monetary constraints, there should have been no surprise that the behavior exhibited has been highly erratic. Any other pattern would indeed have required more explanation than that which has been observed. From both analysis and observation the ultimate answer to the question concerning "successful" policy activism in this model, as in the others examined, must be negative.

7. Nonbenevolent and Monolithic Agent Divorced from Electoral Constraints but Subject to Legal-Constitutional Rules Against Personal Enrichment but Also to Constitutional Rules That Direct Policy Action

The generally negative answer to the question posed in the title prompts examination of still other institutional structures that do not involve attempts at "policy activism," as such, but which, instead, embody sets of predictable and directed policy actions in accordance with constitutionally specified rules. In familiar terminology, if "policy activism," when applied in a setting of *discretionary authority*, must fail to meet the success criterion, can a setting of *rules* do better? It would be inappropriate to discuss at length the relative advantages of alternative regimes or sets of rules. But it is clear that almost any well-defined set of rules would eliminate most of the incentive and motivational sources for the failure of discretionary agency models as previously discussed.

In a very real sense there is no agency problem in an effectively operating rule-ordered regime. A fiscal–monetary authority, charged with the actual implementation of policy, but only in the carrying out of specified rules, defined either in terms of means or objectives, cannot itself be judged on other than purely administrative criteria of success or failure. More ultimate criteria must now be applied to the alternative sets of rules, with success or failure accordingly assigned. And working models of such alternative sets might be analyzed, just as the models of a discretionary agency have been analyzed here. But there seems to be a closer relationship between the rules that might be selected and the success criterion adopted than there is between the latter and the pronounced goals of a discretionary agency.

The potential for success of rule-guided macropolicy depends, in large part, on the *absence* of policy activism, not only for the removal of the potential for self-interested behavior on the part of discretionary agents, but also for the built-in predictability of such action that is inherent in the notion of rules, as such. The relative advantages of rule-guided policy over agency discretion could be treated at length, but this effort would carry me well beyond my assignment in this paper.

8. Fiscal Policy and Monetary Policy

There are two distinct policy instruments, or sets of instruments, in both the familiar textbook terminology and, indeed, in the overall subject of this conference: fiscal policy instruments and monetary policy instruments. To this point I have made no distinction between these two sets, and I have avoided altogether any discussion of relative efficacy as well as relative vulnerability to the sorts of influences on behavior that are emphasized in a public-choice approach. It is time to explore some of the differences that are directly relevant to the arguments that I have advanced.

Fiscal policy involves budgetary manipulation and, hence, a necessary linkage between any macropolicy objectives and the whole process of public-sector allocation. Given this necessary linkage, and given the institutional–political history, it seems totally unreal to suggest that any shift of authority over fiscal policy would be delegated to either discretionary or even to rule-bound authority. It seems highly unlikely that fiscal policy, in any sense, would be removed from the ordinary procedures of democratic decision making, with divided legislative and executive responsibilities and roles in its overall formulation. It becomes unrealistic in the extreme to presume that we, in the United States, would transfer to an agency immune from electoral constraints any authority to manipulate either side of the budget in accordance with rules or intentions to improve macroeconomic performance. Decisions on tax rates, spending rates, and, in consequence, deficits and borrowing requirements, are likely to remain within the responsibility of "democratic" determination, with the predicted result that any meaningful success criterion will fail to be satisfied. There will be a bias toward "easy budgets," with higher-than-desired deficits, to the extent that any considerations of macroeconomic policy enter the policy argument.[4]

Given this predicted bias, and quite apart from any consideration as to the independent efficacy of budgetary policy in effectuating desired results, any genuine hope for "success" in macroeconomic policy must involve a reduction or removal of budgetary manipulation from the potentially usable kit of tools.[5] If "fiscal policy" can be isolated so as to insure that its operation does not make the task of monetary management more difficult, a major step toward genuine reform will have been made. It is in this context that the argument for a constitutional rule requiring budget balance becomes important in macroeconomic policy discussion.

If fiscal policy is so isolated, the task of policy action is left to the monetary agency or regime. A monetary agency can be made effective if the discretion of the agent is limited by the imposition of legally binding and enforcible rules for policy actions. These rules may take on any one of several forms, and it would be out of place to discuss these alternatives in detail here. The monetary agency can be directed to act on the defined monetary aggregates so as to insure prespecified quantity targets (as in some Friedman-like growth rule). Or the authority might be directed to act so as to achieve a specifically defined outcome target, such as the maintenance of stability in the value of the monetary unit. In either case the structure of the rules must be such as to invoke penalities for the failure of the authorities to act in accordance with the declared norms. Some allowance for within-threshold departures from targeted objectives would, of course, be necessary.

But only with some such feedbacks in place can the persons in positions of responsibility as monetary agents be expected to perform so as to further the success criterion that is implicit in the imposition of the rules. It seems at least conceptually possible to build in a workable reward–penalty structure for the compensation and employment of rule-bound monetary agents. And, in the limiting case, such a reward–penalty structure, appropriately related to the achievement of the desired policy target, may obviate the need for explicit definition of a rule for policy action. For example, if the compensations of all employees of the monetary authority should be indexed so as to insure personal penalty from any departures from monetary stability, perhaps nothing more need be required by way of rules. (Such a scheme might involve the maintenance of fixed nominal salary levels against inflation, and double indexing of salaries against deflation, or some more sophisticated formulae.)

If no incentive–motivational structure is deemed to be institutionally and politically feasible, under the operation of any fiat money regime, the argument for more basic regime shift in the direction of an automatic or self-correcting system based on some commodity base is substantially strengthened. The relative advantage of all such systems lies in their incorporation of market-like incentives to generate behavior that will tend to generate at least long-term stability in the value of the monetary unit.

9. Conclusion

In this discussion, as elsewhere, the primary implication of public-choice theory is that institutional–constitutional change or reform is required to achieve ultimate success in macroeconomic policy. There is relatively little to be gained by advancing arguments for "better informed" and "more public-spirited" agents, to be instructed by increasingly sophisticated "economic consultants" who are abreast of the frontiers of the "new science." All such effort will do little more than provide employment for those who are involved. It is the *political economy of policy* that must be reformed. Until and unless this step is taken, observed patterns of policy outcomes will continue to reflect accurately the existing political economy within which these outcomes are produced. And we shall continue to have conferences and discussions about the failures of "policy activism."

Notes

1. For further elaboration and analysis, see Geoffrey Brennan and James Buchanan (1980) Chap. 6; and (1981).

2. For further elaboration of the analysis, see Geoffrey Brennan and James Buchanan (forthcoming), Chaps. 5 and 6.

3. I shall not develop the argument in support of the contractarian–constitutional criterion for measuring policy success or failure. Let me say only that such a criterion must be used unless we are willing to introduce external and nonindividualistic standards of evaluation.

A more controversial position is the one that suggests that the monetary stability criterion would, indeed, be the one that would emerge from the ideally constructed constitutional setting. I shall not develop the argument in support of this position, although I think it can be plausibly made.

4. For an early statement of this point, see Buchanan (1962). For a more extended discussion, see James M. Buchanan and Richard E. Wagner (1977, 1978).

5. Keynes and the Keynesians must bear a heavy responsibility for destroying the set of classical precepts for fiscal prudence that had operated to keep the natural proclivities of politicians in bounds. By offering what could be interpreted as plausible excuses for fiscal profligacy, modern politicians have, for several decades, been able to act out their natural urges, with the results that we now observe. For further discussion see Buchanan (1984).

References

Brennan, Geoffrey, and James M. Buchanan. 1980. *The Power to Tax*. Cambridge: Cambridge University Press.

————. 1981. *Monopoly in Money and Inflation*. London: Institute of Economic Affairs.

————. n.d. *The Reason of Rules*. Cambridge: Cambridge University Press, forthcoming.

Buchanan, James M. 1962. Easy Budgets and Tight Money. *Lloyds Bank Review*. 64: 17–30.

————. Victorian Budgetary Norms, Keynesian Advocacy and Modern Fiscal Politics. Prepared for Nobel Symposium on Governmental Growth, Stockholm, Sweden, August 1984. Center for Study of Public Choice Working Paper No. 4–02.

Buchanan, James M., and Richard E. Wagner. 1977. *Democracy in Deficit*. New York: Academic Press.

————, eds. 1978. *Fiscal Responsibility in Constitutional Democracy*. Boston: Martinus Nijhoff.

7

An Appeal for Rationality in the Policy Activism Debate

John B. Taylor
STANFORD UNIVERSITY

My assignment for this paper is to provide an up-to-date review of the rational expectations debate about whether activist monetary and fiscal policies can improve macroeconomic performance. Preparing a review is particularly difficult at the present time, because we do not seem to be having much of a debate over policy activism. Looking back over the past five years since I prepared a similar review paper for this conference series [see Taylor (1980)], it now seems to me that the debate about policy effectiveness that raged between rational expectationists and other macroeconomists during the 1970s essentially ended in the early 1980s. Since then, only a few analytical or empirical studies of alternative policy proposals have been conducted, and more importantly little effort has been made to reach agreement among the various proposers, or even delineate specific reasons for disagreement. Clearly a renewal of discussion on these important issues is in order.

Rather than provide a detailed review of an old debate, this paper presents a case and outlines a framework for a new debate about policy. It argues that a good framework for debate is the rational expectations approach to policy evaluation that emerged from the policy ineffectiveness debate of the 1970s, but which has been used far too rarely to study other activist policy issues. The paper includes an outline of the essential aspects of a rational expectations approach to the policy activism question.

1. The End of the Policy Ineffectiveness Debate

Rational expectations first became a big factor in the policy activism debate in the early 1970s when Thomas Sargent and Neil Wallace wrote their famous policy ineffectiveness paper. They showed—using an elementary macroeconomic example based on Robert Lucas's then new model of the Phillips curve—that an active monetary policy could not be effective in stabilizing fluctuations in output and employment. Hence, a monetarist, constant-growth-rate rule for the money supply, such as the one proposed by Milton Friedman years before, was optimal: it could not be improved on by an activist or Keynesian countercyclical stabilization policy.

The Sargent–Wallace paper unsurprisingly ignited a great policy debate. The paper was soon followed up by demonstrations of empirical support for the Lucas model by Sargent and Robert Barro, and extensions of the Lucas model by Barro and others. Almost all Keynesian macroeconomists eventually joined in to register their disagreements. The policy ineffectiveness debate raged for much of the 1970s and completely replaced the monetary–fiscal policy debate among economists in most universities.

The early rational expectations proponents of the policy ineffectiveness view were quite explicit about their analytical framework and the assumptions that formed the underpinnings of their conclusions. For this reason, in my view, the debate had a relatively high degree of rationality compared to many debates about economics. It focused on specific issues of disagreement. In a relatively short period of time, bogus or irrelevant issues had been cast aside and the central reasons for disagreement had been isolated. Empirical tests of the crucial informational assumptions underlying the theory also came surprisingly quickly.

There is little doubt that the excitement surrounding this policy debate was responsible for stimulating the great interest in rational expectations shown by many young macroeconomists during the 1970s. The debate also stimulated thinking about alternatives to Lucas's theory of the Phillips curve—alternatives based on contracts and staggered wage setting with rational expectations in which the policy effectiveness property did not hold. Econometric techniques were improved in order to go beyond the simple Sargent–Wallace-type model and evaluate policy in large and possibly nonlinear models with rational expectations. Much as the monetary–fiscal policy debate, which was ignited by Milton Friedman's original monetarist proposals, generated empirical and theoretical research that improved our understanding of macroeconomic fluctuations, the policy ineffectiveness debate had similar positive fallout.

However beneficial, the policy ineffectiveness debate of the 1970s is now over. There is general agreement that it is the market-clearing assumptions, rather than the rational expectations assumptions, of the Lucas model that are responsible for the policy results; contract models with rational expectations introduced by Edmund Phelps, Stanley Fischer, myself, and others imply that policies that react to the state of the economy can improve macroeconomic performance. These contract models are now as much a part of rational expectations as the market-clearing models. In his textbook Michael Parkin (1984) has accordingly divided up the rational expectations school into two parts: the "new classical" school and the "new Keynesian" school. There also seems to be general agreement that the empirical support for the Lucas new classical model is weaker than the early Barro and Sargent studies showed. There is also general agreement that the new Keynesian models with rational expectations need some bolstering of their microeconomic foundations. Of course, others might characterize these areas of agreement somewhat differently. [See the survey by McCallum (1980) or a more recent one by myself (1985) for details and references.]

2. The Current Deadlock

One might have expected (as I did) that when the controversy over the policy ineffectiveness issue became resolved, rational expectations researchers in macroeconomics would then turn to other important, though perhaps less exotic, issues in the policy activism debate. Although there was agreement that the constant-growth-rate rule is not necessarily optimal, there still was relatively little agreement or even discussion about what a better rule might look like. Reflecting on the policy effectiveness debate, Stanley Fischer (1980, 226) noted, "After all, we do not know the optimal activist policy." There are many other issues to be resolved: how would we implement an activist policy rule if that would improve macroeconomic performance? Karl Brunner (1981) has raised questions about this practical issue. Can one deal in practice with the serious problem of lags and uncertainty in the effect of policy that the proponents of constant-growth-rate rules emphasize? Milton Friedman (1984) still feels that this is the fundamental problem with activist policy:

> . . . slow, steady, monetary growth. That is not a necessary implication of monetarist theory. A believer in monetarist theory still can favor an activist monetary policy as a way to offset other changes in the economy. . . . [however] the monetary authorities have typically made matters worse. . . . they have been a source of uncertainty and instability in the economy.

These are important areas of controversy in the policy activism debate that have not been resolved and about which there is little consensus or agreement. Yet serious research and evaluation of alternative policy rules using the rational expectations techniques that proved useful in resolving the earlier issues (or, for that matter, using any other analytical framework) is not underway at anything like the scale of research that we saw in the policy ineffectiveness debate. The policy activism debate has not moved in the direction that one would have thought.

I am not sure why this is so. Perhaps the apparent political success of supply-side economics discouraged those who thought scientific research in economics could have a hearing among policymakers. Perhaps the costly 1980–82 disinflation disillusioned some enthusiasts of the rational expectations assumption, though I do not feel it should have. Perhaps constant talk of budget deficits has made it difficult to concentrate on discussions about policy activism or made one feel terribly impractical in searching for long-run policy reforms.

Of course, policy talk has not stopped, and there have been interesting proposals for new, and not so new, policy rules to replace the monetarist constant-growth-rate rule: price rules, nominal GNP rules, interest-rate rules, gold-standard rules. Indeed there is now more talk and proposing than ever. The problem, in my view, is that there has been little attempt to evaluate these proposals within a theoretical or empirical framework that is specific enough to be criticized, debated, and eventually used to resolve disagreements.

This no-debate situation is troublesome at a time when there is a clear need for some consensus among macroeconomists. Lester Thurow (1983, xv) expresses what is probably a commonly felt view: "The current intellectual disarray among economists is matched only by a parallel time of confusion during the early days of the Great Depression." The old Keynesian consensus is clearly gone, but nothing has yet replaced it. The lack of such a consensus leaves the economy vulnerable to economic policy actions based on little theoretical or empirical support. In his recent book on policy Herbert Stein (1984, 324) expresses the situation more passionately but no less accurately:

> Although there is much talk about economic policy there is no debate. People say what they have always believed, or what they find it convenient to say, but there is no confrontation of the arguments. There is no effort to find the sources of disagreement or to reach agreement, perhaps because the participants think that the effort to change minds and reach agreement is hopeless. Talk about economic policy has become only a way of rallying one's own troops.

3. What Is the Rational Expectations Approach?

If the rational expectations approach is to provide a suitable framework for debating policy, it is necessary to have a general understanding of the approach. Despite numerous conferences and survey papers, there is still great confusion—especially among noneconomists and economists outside universities—about what the rational expectations approach to policy is. Consider, therefore, the following five general principles that I think summarize the rational expectations approach to macroeconomics.

First, people are forward-looking, and their future expectations can be modeled reasonably accurately by assuming that they have learned the basic statistical regularities of the business cycle, and they use this information to make unbiased (but not error-free) forecasts.

This, of course, is just the Muth definition of rational expectations applied to macroeconomics. It seems like a reasonable assumption for macroeconomic applications because many features of economic fluctuations are recurrent from one business cycle to another; there are established statistical regularities. Since business cycles have been observed for hundreds of years, it makes sense to assume that people have become familiar with them. Such a forward-looking unbiased forecasting assumption would not be reasonable for new unprecedented events for which there is no experience.

Second, macroeconomic policy should be stipulated and evaluated as a rule, rather than as one-time changes in the policy instruments.

Because people are assumed to be forward-looking, their expectations of future policy actions affect their current behavior and the state of the economy. Hence, in order to evaluate the effect of policy on the economy, we need to specify not only current policy changes but also future policy changes. In other words we need to specify a contingency plan that describes how policy will react to future events. Such a contingency is nothing more than a rule for policy. Of course, the contingency plan could specify a constant-growth-rate rule for the money supply, but more generally there will be some reaction from the state of the economy.

The rational expectations approach forces one to think about policy as a rule or a strategy. Once you are working with a rational expectations model, you soon realize that you have little choice but to specify policy as a rule. My own experience is that I have naturally specified policy rules in rational expectations policy evaluation studies without much thought about it one way or the other. This practical reason for thinking about policy as a rule does not seem to have been mentioned in the early discussions of rules versus discretion, but it does support the case for rules over discretion.

Note that the focus on rules does not mean that the effect of one-shot changes in policy should never be calculated with a rational expectations model. Such a calculation can be a useful thought experiment to help understand the workings of the model, but it is, of course, necessary to specify whether the change is anticipated or unanticipated, as well as whether it is temporary or permanent.

The famous critique of econometric policy evaluation put forth by Robert Lucas (1976) is the technical side of this principle. Lucas showed that traditional econometric models would give incorrect answers to policy evaluation problems if expectations were forward-looking and there was a change in the policy rule. Since these traditional models were based on adaptive backward-looking expectations, their parameters would change when the policy rule changed. This was the negative part of the critique and has clearly made policy analysts wary of using the traditional models. But there was also a positive side. The Lucas critique provided a general framework for modifying the traditional models; by stipulating policy as a rule it is possible to calculate by how much the parameters of the traditional models would change. Much technical econometric research by Thomas Sargent, Lars Hansen, and others has been devoted to developing such a framework.

Christopher Sims (1982) has recently argued that the focus of the rational expectations approach on alternative policy rules is irrelevant. He argues that we rarely get big changes in rules anyway, so that we might as well use reduced forms or conventional econometric models for policy. It is true that there is a utopian flavor to the rational expectations approach. The search is for big policy reforms that would improve economic welfare over a long period of time. The reforms would probably require changes in the policy-making institutions or the creation of new institutions. Such reforms are, by their very nature, rare. But they do occur. The creation of the Federal Reserve System, the departure from the gold standard, and the shift to floating exchange rates are all examples. These reforms seem to have had substantial effects on the economy. A careful analysis of the effects of future policy reforms therefore seems quite relevant.

Third, in order to get the benefits of a particular policy rule, it is necessary to establish a commitment to that rule.

As was first pointed out by Finn Kydland and Edward Prescott (1977), dynamic models with rational expectations can lead to problems of time inconsistency. They discovered this problem while attempting to compute optimal policy along the lines suggested by Lucas. In a dynamic model of investment and in a Phillips curve model, they found that once policymakers began on an optimal policy there was incentive in future periods for the policymakers to change the plan—to be inconsistent. Policymakers could make things better by being inconsistent. This was true even if the welfare function of policymakers was identical to that of people in the economy and did not change over time. However, by being inconsistent the policymakers would be likely to lose credibility; people would begin to assume that the policymakers would change, and this would lead to a new policy-making equilibrium that was generally inferior to the original policy plan of the policymakers. The implication is that to prevent this inferior outcome it is better to maintain a firm commitment to a policy rule.

There is a nice macroeconomic analogy to the macroeconomic time inconsistency problem: patent laws. By promising a patent to inventors, the patent laws stimulate inventive activity. Once a particular invention has been made, however, it is tempting to break the commitment and not give a patent. A policymaker who had the discretion to award patents each year would indeed be tempted not to do so. By holding back the patent, we avoid the economic inefficiencies of a monopoly. Fortunately, reneging on patents does not occur in practice because it is so clear that future inventive activity would suffer. As a result, we have patent laws that limit such discretion. The time inconsistency research suggests that discretion should be limited for similar reasons in macroeconomic policy. It should be emphasized that evaluating policy as a rule does not prevent time inconsistency. There still may be temptation to change the rule. The commitment to the rule is the important feature of this third principle.

The previous two principles together imply that a rational expectations analysis of "activist" policies is actually an analysis of policy *rules with feedback* from the state of the economy to the policy instruments. There is a big distinction between "discretionary" and "activist" policies. Those in favor of discretionary policy disagree with the whole concept of a rule-of-the-game approach, whether the rule is a feedback rule or a constant setting for the policy instruments; discretionary policy is formulated on a case-by-case and year-by-year basis with no attempt to commit or even talk about future policy decisions in advance. Activist and constant-growth-rate policy rules have much more in common with each other than do activist policy rules and discretionary policy. Both types of policy rules involve commitments and lead to the type of policy analysis suggested by the rational expectations approach.

The next two principles are related to the types of economic models typically considered by rational expectations economists and to the factors they consider in determining whether a policy is good or not. On these two principles there is more variety among the different departments of the rational expectations school than there is on the first three principles.

Fourth, the economy is basically stable; after a shock the economy will eventually return to its normal trend paths of output and employment.

> *However, because of rigidities in the structure of economy, not in expectation formation, this return may be slow.*

Formal rational expectations models of economic fluctuations are usually *dynamic* systems continually disturbed by stochastic *shocks*. After each shock the economy has a tendency to return to a normal or natural growing level of output and employment, although there may be overshooting or a temporary cumulative movement away from normal. A smooth return is never observed in practice, however, because new shocks are always hitting the system. Since the economy is viewed as always being buffeted around by shocks, rational expectations economists must calculate a "stochastic equilibrium" rather than a "deterministic equilibrium" to describe the behavior of the economy. The combination of the stochastic shocks and the dynamics of rational expectations models is capable of mimicking the actual behavior of business cycles surprisingly well. The properties of the stochastic equilibrium are much like the actual behavior of business cycles.

The shocks can be due to many factors, but they usually have been portfolio preference shocks, productivity shocks, or price shocks. The dynamics are due to many possible rigidities in the economy, but price–wage rigidities and slow adjustment of capital (including inventories) have been the most important empirically.

Because of these rigidities, the impact of a shock to the economy takes time to sort itself out. Suppose, for example, that there is a shift in money velocity with people demanding to hold more money at any level of income and interest rates. Eventually the price level will fall so that the real supply of money is effectively increased. but if there are wage and price rigidities, this adjustment will take time: first the increase in money demand will cause an increase in interest rates; the higher level of interest rates will in turn depress demand for durables and have repercusions throughout the economy; depressed demand conditions will then begin to put downward pressure on prices; the fall in prices then will begin to raise the real supply of money; these prices will continue until the economy is back to its natural level of output and employment. The whole process could take more than a year.

Combined with these structural rigidities is the supposition that expectations are not restrained by similar rigidities. A shock can change expectations of inflation, exchange rates, and other variables overnight, even though there are rigidities that cause the economy to take additional time to fully adjust to the shock. The expectations take account of the structural rigidities, since these are part of the model. This combination of rigidities in the economy with perfectly flexible expectations is an essential feature of most rational expectations models. There has been a tendency to get expectations assumptions mixed up with structural assumptions about how markets work. Hence, the comment that expectations might be rational in flexible auction markets but not in sticky labor markets is frequently heard. These two types of assumptions should be usefully separated. (Again recall that rational expectations are meant to apply to recurrent events, not to unprecedented events. In response to a new event or a new policy rule, slow adjustment of expectations would be likely.)

There has been much research on price and wage rigidities in rational expectations models. The important general feature of this research is that prices and wages have a forward-looking feature, whether they are sticky or not. When workers and firms set wages and prices, they look ahead to the period during which the prices or wages will be in effect—to demand conditions, to the wages of other workers, and so on. This means that expectations of future policy actions will affect wage and price decisions, a property that is quite unlike Keynesian models of wage and price rigidities. The view that the economy will eventually return to normal—however slowly—after a shock is also inconsistent with the Keynesian view of permanent underemployment equilibria.

Fifth, the objective of macroeconomic policy is to reduce the size (or the duration) of the fluctuations of output, employment, and inflation from normal or desired levels after shocks hit the economy. The objective is to be achieved over a long period of time that will, in general, include a large number of business cycle experiences. Future business cycle fluctuations are not viewed as less important than the current one.

By responding to economic shocks in a systematic fashion, economic policy can offset their impact or influence the speed at which the economy returns to normal. It thus can change the size of the fluctuations. How this should be done is a main subject of disagreement among proponents of different policy rules.

From a technical viewpoint the disagreement can be addressed by inserting alternative policy rules into a rational expectations model and calculating how each rule affects the variance of output, employment, and inflation in the stochastic equilibrium that describes the business cycle fluctuations. We want to choose a policy that provides the best economic performance as approximated by this stochastic equilibrium. One simple criterion is the minimization of the variance of output and inflation. Since in many models with price and wage rigidities there will be a trade-off between the reduction of output and inflation variability, it will usually be necessary to stipulate a welfare or loss function that reflects certain value judgments. Frequently, one policy will so dominate another than the particular welfare weights do not matter much, however.

Despite the need to make such value judgments the rational expectations approach is fairly specific about what the objectives of policy should be. Changing the natural or normal levels of output and employment is not the direct objective of stabilization policy from a rational expectations perspective; of course, it is possible that reduced variability of output or inflation could raise the secular growth rate of the economy or reduce the natural rate of unemployment. As a first approximation, these normal levels are not influenced by macroeconomic policy. The secular growth rate of the economy is influenced by tax policy and by the mix between fiscal and monetary policies. But it is the average setting of these instruments rather than their cyclical variations that is most important for long-term growth.

The average rate of inflation can obviously be influenced by monetary policy, and it is important to choose a target rate that maximizes economic welfare. The objective of macroeconomic policy, however, is to keep the inflation rate close to this target rate; that is, to minimize fluctuations around the target, regardless of what the actual value of the target is. Alternatively, if a zero inflation target is appropriate, the objective of policy is to keep the price level near some target; the specific target value itself is much less important.

4. Some Proposals for Activist Policy Rules

Although there have been too few analytical or empirical investigations of activist policy alternatives to monetarist rules, there clearly have been some. Mention of a few here may serve as a departure for discussion. I restrict myself to proposals being investigated by two of my macroeconomist colleagues at Stanford, Robert Hall (1984) and Ronald McKinnon (1984), as well as myself. Since the proposals are not exactly alike, there is room for discussion, and the examples are obviously not offered here as the final word.

4.1. An elastic price rule

Hall (1984) considers a policy rule in which the Fed manipulates its policy instruments in order to keep the deviations of the price level from its target level equal to eight times the deviation of the unemployment rate from its target level. The figure eight is chosen as an example; more generally, the exact number would be chosen after public discussion. The objective of the proposal is to stabilize *fluctuations* in both unemployment and the aggregate price. The *level* of unemployment rate is taken as given and equal to the natural rate. Equivalently, the policy attempts to establish an aggregate demand curve (in price-output space) that is steeper than a monetary rule or a nominal GNP rule and thereby less tolerant of output fluctuations than a monetarist rule.

Clearly this proposal fits into the policy evaluation framework outlined in the previous section. The emphasis is on cyclical fluctuations over a long period of time, the target level of unemployment is assumed to be unaffected by policy, and the policy evaluated is a rule. Discretion is not completely eliminated, however, because the Fed must decide the appropriate instrument setting to achieve the rule, but Hall does consider the problems of stating the rule in terms of magnitudes that the Fed does not directly control. The policy is evaluated by using a dynamic stochastic framework like that described under principle 4.

4.2. An exchange rate rule

McKinnon (1984) has been investigating an activist policy rule in which the Fed increases the growth rate of the money supply whenever the dollar exchange rate appreciates (relative to some target) against other hard currencies, particularly the mark and the yen. A lower exchange rate calls for a reduction of the money growth rate. Similarly the rule calls for the Bundesbank and the Bank of Japan to increase the growth rates of their money supplies whenever their exchange rates appreciate. In this sense the rule involves policy coordination between the countries. There is also coordination in maintaining agreement on the long-run trend path of the world money supply or at least the group money supply for the United States, Germany and Japan.

This exchange rate rule is designed to offset portfolio preference shocks that McKinnon views as arising partly via currency substitution between countries, and his analytical framework is directed toward such shocks. Although rational expectations is not entered explicitly into this framework, the quick movement of forward-looking exchange rate expectations in the face of rigidities elsewhere in the economy is one of the motivations behind focusing policy on the exchange rate.

4.3. An activist money-supply rule

In my own research I have investigated the properties of an activist money-supply rule that reacts to the state of the economy. Although a complex optimal rule was calculated for a particular rational expectations model using the overall approach outlined here, that rule turned out to be remarkably similar to a simpler rule in which the growth of the money supply is increased whenever real output is below its trend growth target; and by a little bit more when output is falling relative to its trend growth target. As a close approximation, the rule involved no accommodation of the money supply to inflation shocks. Hence, monetary policy has a stabilization role but no accommodation role. According to this framework this specific activist rule would work better than a monetarist rule.

An alternative to this proposal would have the stabilization role of monetary policy given over to a fiscal policy rule similar to the automatic stabilizers. This would make the monetary authorities responsible only for maintaining a fixed money-growth rate, which could reduce temptation to accommodate inflation. It would also prevent monetary policy from having international repercussions when attempting to react to domestic policy disturbances. However, allocation of all stabilization policy to a fiscal policy rule might require some explicit attempt to deal with interest-sensitive investment demand.

5. Concluding Remarks

My aim here has been to present a rational expectations framework within which a number of issues in the policy activism controversy might be fruitfully discussed and debated. The hope is that such a framework might bring more rationality to a debate that now seems to be in a slump. The framework involves a number of specific features that I think are reasonable and on which there might be some agreement, but it is by no means a straitjacket. It leaves plenty of interesting modeling questions open to the investigator of a particular problem.

References

Brunner, Karl. 1981. The case against policy activism. *Lloyds Bank Review* No. 139.

Fischer, Stanley. 1980. On activist monetary policy with rational expectations. In *Rational Expectations and Economic Policy*, ed. S. Fischer. Chicago: University of Chicago Press.

Friedman, Milton. 1984. Has monetarism failed? *Manhattan Report* 4: No. 3. New York: Manhattan Institute for Policy Research.

Hall, Robert E. 1984. Monetary strategy with an elastic price standard. Federal Reserve Bank of Kansas City Conference on Monetary Policy.

Kydland, Finn, and Edward C. Prescott. 1977. Rules rather than discretion: The inconsistency of optimal plans. *Journal of Political Economy* 85: 473–91.

Lucas, Robert E., Jr. 1976. Econometric policy evaluation: A critique. *Carnegie–Rochester Conference Series of Public Policy*, Vol. 1. Amsterdam: North-Holland.

_____ 1980. Rules, discretion, and the role of the economic advisor. In *Rational Expectations and Economic Policy*, ed. S. Fischer. Chicago: University of Chicago Press.

McCallum, Bennett T. 1980. Rational expectations and macroeconomic stabilization policy: An overview. *Journal of Money, Credit and Banking* 12: 716–46.

McKinnon, Ronald I. 1984. *An International Standard for Monetary Stabilization.* Washington, D.C.: The Institute for International Economics. (Distributed by M.I.T. Press.)

Parkin, Michael. 1984. *Macroeconomics.* Englewood Cliffs, N.J.: Prentice-Hall.

Sims, Christopher. 1982. Policy making with econometric models. *Brookings Papers on Economic Activity* 1.

Stein, Herbert. 1983. *Presidential Economics: The Making of Economic Policy from Roosevelt to Reagan and Beyond.* New York: Simon and Schuster.

Taylor, John B. 1980. Recent developments in the theory of stabilization policy. *Stablization Policy: Lessons for the 1970's and Implications for the 1980's,* ed. L. Meyer. Federal Reserve Bank of St. Louis.

_____ 1981. Stabilization, accommodation, and monetary rules. *American Economic Review* 70: 145–49.

_____ n.d. Rational expectations models in macroeconomics. In *Frontiers in Economics,* ed. K. Arrow and S. Honkapojha. Oxford: Basil Blackwell. Forthcoming.

Thurow, Lester. 1983. *Dangerous Currents: The State of Economics.* New York: Random House.

Index

Contributing Authors

ALAN S. BLINDER is Professor of Economics, Princeton University, Princeton, New Jersey 08544.

KARL BRUNNER, Director of the Center for Research in Government Policy and Business, is also Professor of Economics, University of Rochester, Rochester, New York 14627.

JAMES M. BUCHANAN, who is Director, Center for Study of Public Choice, is Professor of Economics, George Mason University, Fairfax, Virginia 22030.

ROBERT J. GORDON is Professor of Economics, Northwestern University, Evanston, Illinois 60201.

R.W. HAFER is Research Officer at the Federal Reserve Bank of St. Louis, St. Louis, Missouri 63166.

BENNETT T. McCALLUM is Professor of Economics, Carnegie-Mellon University, Pittsburgh, Pennsylvania 15213.

JOHN B. TAYLOR is Professor of Economics, Stanford University, Stanford, California 94305.